LIFE-COACH YOURSELF TO SUCCESS

BARRIE PEARSON
NEIL THOMAS

THOROGOOD

Thorogood Publishing
10-12 Rivington Street
London EC2A 3DU
Telephone: 020 7749 4748
Fax: 020 7729 6110
Email: info@thorogoodpublishing.co.uk
Web: www.thorogoodpublishing.co.uk

A CIP catalogue record for this book is available from the British Library.

ISBN PB: 978 185418 9318
ISBN Ebook: 978 185418 9325

Designed by Driftdesign Ltd

Barrie Pearson

For Catherine, the love of my life, for her children and especially for her grandchildren

Neil Thomas

For Cheryl, Amy and Ella

The authors

Barrie Pearson (writes his co-author) is a truly inspirational individual – a natural communicator (and successful seminar presenter) and, after great experience as a senior executive with multinational companies, a successful entrepreneur. He founded a corporate finance boutique – Livingstone Guarantee plc, the first independent corporate finance house in the UK, advising on acquisitions, disposals, management buy-ins and buy-outs, flotations and corporate finance. He sold the company for a substantial sum. He then created a new business called Realization, dedicated to world class mentoring and coaching for successful entrepreneurs and chief executives in wealth creation and personal development. The lessons in this book have been tested throughout his business and private life.

Neil Thomas has, after working for various media companies, also built and sold a training business (the seminar, training and publishing business, Hawksmere plc) and then a magazine business. He is currently involved in a variety of business ventures, including Falconbury Ltd and Management Forum Ltd, both seminar and training companies.

Barrie Pearson and Neil Thomas have each written several books, but their only other jointly authored work was the international best-selling *The Shorter MBA*. Neil has also written a wide range of fiction books: www.neilthomasauthor.com.

Barrie Pearson has lived his life according to the approaches outlined in this book and Neil Thomas constantly aspires, sometimes successfully, to do the same, but for him, the road to success is always under construction.

Contents

Introduction

We all take ourselves for granted. We make plans for **other people.** We solve **their problems.** We make profits for **them.** We think strategically at work and not at home. We build businesses for our companies and not for ourselves. We know the value of our house and we know the rate of return on money we invest, yet we do not put a value on ourselves as individuals or as income-producers. This book will put a stop to this.

It is not a charter for selfishness, but it is unashamedly a manual to help you realise your full potential – by putting yourself first for a change – in assessing your assets and skills, in deciding what you want to achieve both personally and professionally and in moving you along the path of life as if it is indeed the road to success.

You must assess whether your life is on track. In asking yourself if you are living the life you would like to be leading, start by using the well-known technique of writing your own 'ideal' obituary. Now ask yourself how wide is the divergence between the way you would like your life to go and the way it is currently shaping up. See the problem? Let this book help you to get back on track.

We are firmly of the view that *you* can be the best business you will ever get to manage, but only if you take stock of yourself and act to exploit your skills, interests and personality. Remember, the success you take is equal to the plans you make.

How to use this book

The book is a combination of informative narrative and self-assessment questionnaires to help you decide the practical action needed to change your life.

It is divided into these main sections:

Part one: Here's looking at **you**

This encourages you to put yourself first and examines how to:

- take stock of your assets by giving yourself a personal MOT
- manage your finances and create personal wealth
- take control of your own life by setting goals, asking yourself 'whose life is it anyway?'

before moving on to:

- reviewing and identifying the skills which you need to develop to achieve successful personal and economic results.

Part two: The business end – me at work and me plc

This looks at your working life either as an employee:

- my brilliant career;

or as an entrepreneur:

- starting your own business.

Part three: Knowing me, knowing you

This focuses on understanding yourself and others:

- hell is other people;

and how best to:

- manage your health;

and how to:

- get your family and friend relationships right.

Part four: Action planning: DIY and do it now

This is where you are encouraged to prescribe actions so that goals become an:

- action plan

and that you reinvent yourself with:

- the new you – a personal vision statement.

Appendix: 'Touchstones' – habits and traits of the successful

This offers, in summary form, 'touchstones' which are key habits and traits of successful individuals under the headings:

- career
- health
- relationships
- personal finances
- mental attitudes
- image and appearance
- entrepreneurs.

PART ONE: HERE'S LOOKING AT **YOU**

one

CHAPTER

01

TAKE STOCK OF YOUR ASSETS: CARRY OUT A PERSONAL MOT

01

Introduction

Be honest. You are reading this book because you want to improve some aspects of your life. If you work at it, this book will help you improve your life dramatically, but it does require you to be frank with yourself from the outset.

Before you can set achievable self-improvement goals and draw up an action plan designed to make them a reality, you need to take stock of your assets and to identify what is holding you back. We regard it as carrying out a personal MOT. Throughout this chapter there are self assessment questionnaires which you need to complete. Just thinking about it in your mind is simply not disciplined enough to get the results you want. But don't jump ahead of yourself by starting to fill in the questionnaires without reading each part of this chapter first.

You need to read this chapter to gain the insight required before you can carry out an effective personal assessment, but first just to show that we take better care of our motor cars than we do of ourselves, we give an example of how a fun personal MOT could look, then we invite you to test in detail these key elements of your life:

- work and career
- health
- relationships
- personal finances
- leisure and holidays
- appearance and image
- mental attitudes
- qualifications, skills and personal development
- direction and goals.

A Personal MOT

1 Age	59
2 Date of last 'test' When did you last think carefully about your life and plans?	3/3/21
3 Engine size and condition Is your brain regularly stimulated and tuned up at work and/or play and is your mental health good?	Yes/No
4 Bodywork Do you exercise regularly? Have you let yourself go?	 Yes/No Yes/No
5 Capital value Do you know your value on the open market? – Salary/earnings – Net assets Now gross up your salary/earnings at prevailing rate of interest* to find out how much capital you would have to have invested to yield a return equal to your salary/earnings, eg (salary/*say 2%) x 100 = capital value of:	 £ 15 [illegible] £ 0 £ 3,00
6 Brakes What if anything is holding you back and preventing you from realising your goals? On the other hand, do you have the mechanism to stop yourself doing the things that can ruin your life (the addictions of drink, drugs, smoking and gambling)?	Mentoring support £ 6
7 Optional extras Do you have valuable skills? Or are you a bog-standard worker with no extras?	 Yes/No Yes/No

8 Steering and navigation system

Are you driving the machine? Yes/No

Do you know where you're going? Yes/No

9 What essential repairs are needed to make you truly roadworthy?

List what you need to do (to include skills development and goal setting):

- Need to pass QTLS Exam ASAP.
- Need to hire a advertise company
- Need to learn how to grow my B.
- and apply.
- Need to learn more about MLM doTerra.
- Improve my Self Image.

Work and career

It is not enough to have a job or even a job and a career. For some people their job is the problem and you should evaluate it and your career prospects under the following headings:

Enjoyment and stress

Ask yourself:

- are you happy in your job?
- what parts of your job do you really enjoy and which parts cause you stress?
- do you like working for the company you are with?

Learning and self development

Record:

- job related skills you have learned
- general skills you have developed which are transportable, e.g. effective writing, time management, social media engagement
- additional qualifications you have obtained with company help, or available opportunities you could pursue, e.g. a part-time or distance learning MBA
- job rotation experience you have obtained or could pursue

Networking opportunities

Ask yourself and record:

- what networking opportunities are available? With customers and suppliers or via trade association functions, lecturing opportunities at industry conferences etc.
- how systematically have you pursued these opportunities?

Promotion prospects

Ask yourself:

- have you reached an effective glass ceiling for whatever reason?
- how quickly and how far have other people been promoted from your position?
- is the company creating additional promotion opportunities? Or stagnating? Or even downsizing?

Hours worked

Record and ask yourself:

- how many hours per week do you work and additionally spend travelling?
- why do you do so much overtime?
- do you simply work late because other people do?
- what would happen if you worked much less overtime?
- do you take an effective lunch break?

Basic income

Is your basic income:

- enough to cover your monthly expenditure?!
- comparable with what other companies pay? Check job adverts and talk to relevant recruitment agencies to get an accurate view.
- more in thousands than your age? E.g. earning more than £25,000 at 25?
- comparable with other people in the company, taking into account age, qualifications, experience and contribution?

Overtime payments, bonuses and profit share

Do you receive:

- paid overtime? Even some major professional firms pay overtime to junior professional staff as well as to support staff
- an additional bonus at periodic intervals? Does it reward personal effort and achievement adequately and fairly?
- a profit share payment? Is it really a percentage of profits or a discretionary bonus in disguise?

Share options

Ask yourself:

- when are you likely to receive share options, how many and how much could they be worth after what length of time?
- if you leave the company, do your options become worthless?

Equity ownership prospects

Ask yourself:

- are you eligible to join an employee share savings scheme and how much capital could you accumulate by when?
- if you work for a private company, is there likely to be an opportunity to buy or acquire shares from the owners on attractive terms?
- if the owners are approaching retirement, or you work for a subsidiary of a group which is likely to become non-core, is there likely to be a realistic opportunity to pursue a management buy-out?

Risk and vulnerability

Ask yourself:

- do you work for an individual or company prone to dismiss people arbitrarily and abruptly?
- is the company in decline, possibly facing receivership or vulnerable to a takeover?
- how adequate is your leaving package? Would it pay you to stay on, be dismissed or made redundant?

Overall assessment

Sum up your job and career prospects in the following terms:

- you are content and happy, so you should stay for the foreseeable future
- you are happy, but underpaid, and should seek an improvement
- you should look around in a measured way
- you need to leave quickly to avoid dismissal or simply to protect your health or save your marriage
- you can happily imagine doing the same job/being with the same company in 5 years'/10 years'/20 years' time?

Now you are ready to complete the work and career questionnaire.

WORK AND CAREER

Name ____

Date ____

Basic income ______________________________________

Overtime payments, bonuses and profit share ________________

Promotion prospects _________________________________

Hours worked ______________________________________

Enjoyment and stress ________________________________

Learning and self development _________________________

Networking opportunities _____________________________

Share options ______________________________________

Equity ownership prospects ___________________________

Risk and vulnerability _______________________________

Overall assessment __________________________________

Health

We all tend to take good health for granted until we have a problem. By then it could be too late. Don't even think that you are too young to have a health problem or to be at risk, because the evidence is overwhelmingly against you. 'Healthy' people are diagnosed with cancer in their twenties, or become alcoholics or have a mental breakdown which derails their career.

This section of the book has been written from the twin standpoints of common sense and balance, but it is firmly based on accepted medical knowledge. Evaluate your own health under the following headings:

Exercise

Exercise is fundamental to good health and helps to promote mental health as well. One of the most effective antidotes to pressure and stress is exercise. When you are taking physical exercise, it is amazing how you will forget about pressure and stress, at least temporarily.

Use an app (or record) and ask yourself:

- how often do you exercise sufficiently to break into a sweat?
- what are your excuses for not playing team games, working out at the gym, joining an exercise class, doing regular exercises at home, buying an exercise bicycle or rowing machine?

Sleep

Adequate sleep is central to good health, effective performance at work and avoiding accidents when driving. Mrs Thatcher attracted plenty of press coverage for only requiring four or five hours sleep a night, but perhaps she took catnaps as well, much as Winston Churchill did. The overwhelming majority of people will benefit from having seven or eight hours sleep a night, which allows the body to effectively regenerate itself and helps to ward off illness. It may be considered macho to boast about burning the candle at both ends by working and playing excessively hard, but the result is damaging to your health and the effectiveness of your mind.

Ask yourself:

- how many hours sleep a night and each week do you get?
- do you have difficulty getting to sleep or do you wake up in the middle of the night thinking about problems? This could be a tangible signal of stress which left unchecked may lead to a mental breakdown.
- do you take sleeping pills regularly, or even occasionally? Recognise that some sleeping pills can quickly become addictive.
- if you have problems sleeping, how much fresh air and exercise do you take?

Alcohol

Alcohol is enjoyable within sensible limits, but it has the power to steal up on you and take over your life. Yes, the medical profession seems agreed that one or two glasses of wine a day, especially red, can be good for your health and indeed better than total abstinence. The message about alcohol is enjoy it in moderation, and the best advice about drinking and driving is – don't! There seems to be some differences of opinion within the medical profession, but sensible weekly limits seem to be 14 units for women and for men, based on a unit of a medium-sized glass of wine or a half pint of beer or lager. Tell-tale signs of alcohol dependence include needing a drink every day and thinking about how soon you are going to have your first drink of the day. A sensible way of ensuring you are in control of alcohol is to have at least one alcohol free day a week, and occasionally to have an alcohol free week or even month. If you suspect you are drinking more than the recommended limit, then beware of the attitude that says you can handle it anyway, so what. That's exactly how dependency takes hold insidiously.

Ask yourself and record:

- how many units you drink each week over, say, a period of a few weeks
- do you think ahead to when your first drink of the day will be?
- how often do you say to yourself 'I need a drink or I deserve a drink'?
- when did you last have an alcohol free day or week?

Weight

Your weight is important, and not just for your health. Being overweight is bad for your heart and may well cause problems with your joints in later life. If you are still young, then your response may be your weight doesn't matter because you are not at risk yet. The reality is, however, that as the years go by it becomes harder and less likely that you will lose weight.

Excess weight may work against you in other ways. Some employers are prejudiced against excess weight, perhaps wrongly assuming that it is a sign of laziness or that it does not fit the 'corporate image'. Unfair, but it could adversely affect your getting the job you want. Equally, excess weight may work against you attracting the partner you want.

Anorexia is a harmful condition, and medical opinion suggests that it is associated with a form of mental illness. Once anorexia takes hold it can be damaging and lasting. So the key to prevention is to reject the mental attitude that being ultra slim is a desirable goal and to recognise the early signs of anorexic behaviour.

Ask yourself and record:

- what is your weight and height?
- are you over or underweight?
- is your weight increasing or decreasing significantly?
- be honest, are you prone to bingeing or starving?

Your body mass index (BMI) gives an indication of your weight in relation to your height. It's a general guide only – acceptable levels are determined by your sex, build, or amount of muscle. See your GP if you're worried that your weight may be affecting your health.

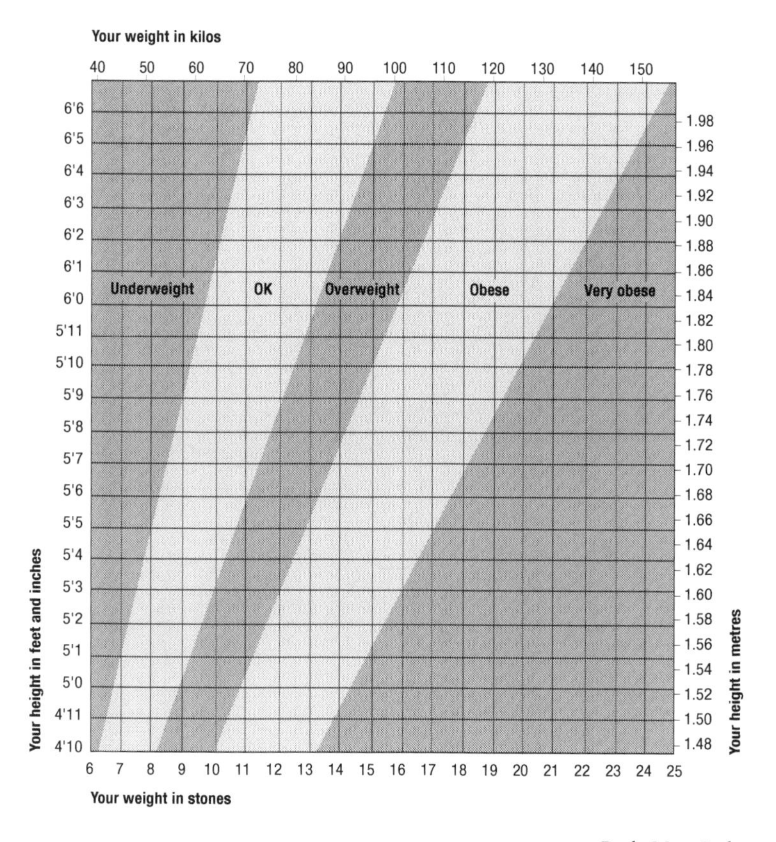

Body Mass Index

Stress

Arguably stress is in the mind, but that does not make it any less real. Acceptable levels of stress are quite beneficial and help people perform better. Stress is very personal – what is unbearably stressful to someone may be stimulating to others. Undue stress can lead to a situation which threatens your health, your career in the short-term and your relationship with your partner. Signs of undue stress must be recognised.

Ask yourself and record:

- what is causing you stress at work and at home?
- is it getting worse or better?
- is it affecting your sleep or general well being?
- what needs to change to reduce or eliminate the problem?

Diet

Diet is important at all ages. The ideal time to adopt healthy eating habits is as a small child. Equally, it is never too late, or too soon, to adopt healthy eating habits. The good news is that once adopted, most people find it easy to maintain their healthy eating habits. Cooked breakfasts, burger and chips, cream cakes, crisps and biscuits are enjoyable, but should be regarded as treats. A healthy diet should be built predominantly around vegetables, salads, cereals, pasta, pulses, bread and white meats.

Ask yourself and record:

- how many meals each week do you regard as predominantly healthy or unhealthy?
- what are the unhealthy foods or snacks you are prone to eat?

Smoking

Smoking is dangerous for your health, and the evidence is overwhelming. Simply to reduce your smoking is unacceptable, because despite their best intentions most people soon return to their previous level. There can only be one message, give up smoking as soon as possible. Products such as nicotine patches have helped many people, and your doctor should be ready to offer advice. Vaping (e-cigarettes) can help to quit smoking but is not harm free.

Drugs

Forget the legal, social, medical or even moral arguments, simply reject drugs. There is some evidence that certain soft drugs are neither harmful nor addictive, and progression to harder and more harmful drugs may not happen. So what. Drugs are at best a form of crutch which should be rejected.

Your doctor

There is definite evidence that men are less likely to consult their local doctor than women. Any notion that it is not macho for a man to consult his doctor is nonsense. Whenever you have any symptoms which you are unsure about, the only sensible action is to consult your local doctor.

Health screening

Formal health screening programmes seem to divide medical opinion. Some doctors hold the view that formal health screening reports cause undue worries and concerns. On the other hand, the powerful arguments in favour of formal health screening are that it could provide an early warning of a serious medical condition which requires urgent treatment.

Laughter

An old adage is that laughter is the best medicine but are you becoming one of the great many people who are not even aware that they just aren't laughing anymore? Nowadays there appears to be some medical evidence to suggest that laughter is good for you because it releases minute amounts of beneficial chemicals. Laughter is a sign of well-being.

Ask yourself:

- how often do you laugh at work, at home, with friends and with relatives?

Now complete the health questionnaire.

HEALTH

Name ____________________

Date ____________________

Exercise ____________________

Sleep ____________________

Alcohol ____________________

Weight ____________________

Stress ____________________

Diet ____________________

Other ____________________

____

____

____

____

Relationships

It is human nature to take relationships for granted, but this does not make it right to do so. The importance of relationships becomes starkly obvious at the point of separation, whether it is dismissal at work, being dumped by a partner or feeling desperate to end a relationship. The vital ingredients for effective relationships are time, listening, understanding and effective communication. People who are too busy to spend time on relationships are putting themselves at risk. Time should be invested in relationships – it will pay handsome dividends. Evaluate your own relevant relationships under the following headings:

Partner

Ask yourself:

- how often do you listen and talk together, free from interruption and distraction?
- when you fall out – do you throw blame around, shout and scream, leave differences unresolved, continue to sulk – or make sure that the issue is resolved in an adult way?
- do you always remember birthdays and anniversaries?
- when last did you give an unexpected gift?
- when last did you do something your partner regarded as romantic?
- how would you sum up the state of your relationship?

Children

Ask yourself, and record if appropriate:

- how much time do you spend actually involved with your children? (Watching television in the same room does not count!)
- do you help plan and take part in your children's birthday parties?
- do you make time to attend school functions, parents' evenings, etc.?
- do you work with your partner to instill values, to set guidelines and to exercise discipline when necessary?

Friends

Ask yourself:

- how often do you go out with friends? – how often are you too busy or make excuses?
- do you initiate get-togethers and come up with new venues and activities?
- how many new friends have you made in the past 12 months?
- which friends have you not seen in the past 12 months?
- how often do you invite friends home?
- what have you done to widen your circle of friends?

Work

Ask yourself:

- have you had an appraisal interview in the last six months?
- if not, have you considered asking for an appraisal?

- is your working relationship with your boss friendly, constructive and candid?
- what is the tangible evidence which demonstrates you are a team player?
- how do you interact socially with colleagues during working hours, at lunch and after work?
- do you praise people sincerely and readily?
- do you always say thank you to people, and promptly?
- do you treat junior staff with courtesy and respect?

Interpersonal skills

Ask yourself:

- are you seen as a warm and friendly person? Or stand-offish and pompous, amusing or dull? How do you know you are what you think you are?
- what courses, books or articles have you studied to improve your interpersonal skills?

Now complete the relationships questionnaire.

RELATIONSHIPS

Name ______________________________

Date ______________________________

Partner ______________________________

Children ______________________________

____

Parents ______________________________

____

Friends ______________________________

____

Work ______________________________

____

Interpersonal skills ______________________________

____

Personal finances

The overwhelming majority of people, including the wealthy, want to be wealthier. An awful lot of people, once again including the wealthy, worry about money and find it a cause of stress. Few people really can claim to manage their personal finances outstandingly well, but most people would be significantly better off if they demonstrably improved their own financial management. This area is examined under the following headings:

- personal income and expenditure
- borrowing and debt
- savings
- investments
- pension
- insurance.

Personal income and expenditure

The essential starting point for effective personal financial management is a comparison of income and expenditure. This will reveal if you are slowly but surely getting deeper into debt, or over the course of a year you manage to just about match your income and expenditure, or how much surplus income you have available for treats and indulgences or for investment.

An important classification to make is essential versus discretionary expenditure. Also, intermittent expenditure such as household and car repairs need to be taken into account. With the help of bank and credit card statements, compile an estimated income and expenditure record as follows:

ESTIMATED INCOME AND EXPENDITURE STATEMENT

Date ____

INCOME

	Weekly	Monthly	Quarterly	Half Yearly	Annually
Salary					
Overtime					
Bonus					
Profit Share					
Savings					
Interest					
Dividends					
Other					
TOTAL					

ESSENTIAL EXPENDITURE

	Weekly	Monthly	Quarterly	Half Yearly	Annually
Mortgage payments/ rent					
Council tax/ property taxes					
Heating and lighting					
Water					
Property maintenance					
Food					
Clothes					
Travel to work					
Telephone/IT					
TOTAL					

DISCRETIONARY EXPENDITURE

	Weekly	Monthly	Quarterly	Half Yearly	Annually
Car purchase payments					
Vehicle or road tax					
Car insurance					
Car repairs					
Eating out					
Leisure					
Gifts					
Holidays					
Miscellaneous					
TOTAL					

This basic schedule can easily be translated into total annual income and expenditure using the following schedule:

ESTIMATED ANNUAL INCOME AND EXPENDITURE

Date ______________________________

	Weekly	Monthly	Quarterly	Half Yearly	Annually
INCOME	£ x 52	£ x 12	£ x 4	£ x 2	£ x 1
TOTAL					

ESSENTIAL EXPENDITURE

	Weekly	Monthly	Quarterly	Half Yearly	Annually
INCOME	£ x 52	£ x 12	£ x 4	£ x 2	£ x 1
TOTAL					

DISCRETIONARY EXPENDITURE

	Weekly	Monthly	Quarterly	Half Yearly	Annually
INCOME	£ x 52	£ x 12	£ x 4	£ x 2	£ x 1
TOTAL					

If you have a computer and are familiar with using spreadsheets, you can set up your own spreadsheet and, if you wish, use a separate column for each month which will indicate when your cash outgoings will be at a peak. Smartphone apps can also be useful.

Borrowing and debt

Debt causes stress and worry for many people, and can be a vicious circle because the high cost of interest may push people deeper into debt. Some extended credit purchase terms offered by stores, and their own credit cards, may charge an annual interest rate in the region of 30 per cent. Some credit cards charge a rate of over 20 per cent. annual interest and many banks charge both a fixed fee and a hefty interest rate whenever a current account dips into an unauthorised overdraft. Many people simply do not know the interest rate they are paying or have any accurate idea of how much interest they are paying. A key figure to find out for any borrowing or debt is the Annualised Percentage Rate (APR) because this is the effective rate you are paying, and may be materially higher than the 'interest rate' quoted in large and bold print on advertisements and websites.

The first step in managing your borrowing and debt is to complete the following schedule:

BORROWINGS AND DEBT

Date ____________________

	Amount £	% APR	Monthly Interest Paid
Mortgage			
Loans			
Car			
Home improvement			
Overdraft			
Credit cards			
Other			
TOTAL			

Savings

In addition to a mortgage, some people have both borrowings and savings. Unknown to them, their savings may be costing them money because they would be better off using their savings to reduce their debts. For example, at times banks pay little or nothing in gross interest per annum on current account credit balances, and you may have borrowings costing you between 10 per cent. and 30 per cent. annually.

Some building societies and deposit taking institutions create a new type of account paying an attractive rate of interest, then close that account to new customers, and sharply reduce the rate of interest. To manage your savings effectively, you need to have a schedule of your savings as follows:

SAVINGS

Date ______________________________

	Amount	Gross Interest Rate %	Net Interest Rate %
Current account			
Deposit accounts			
*Cash ISAs (NISAs)			
*National Savings Certificates			
TOTAL			

* denotes tax free savings products available to UK tax payers subject to certain conditions and restrictions

Investments

Investments should be managed effectively – whether you have only £500 invested or many millions is immaterial. People tend to make investments without being aware as to whether or not they are exposing themselves to low, medium or high risk, and how much introductory commission or fees they are paying and to whom. Once again, a simple schedule of investments is needed.

INVESTMENTS

Date ____________________

	Cost £	Date Invested	Value Today £	Gain/Loss £
Shares				
*Equity ISAs				
Other investments				
TOTAL				

* denotes tax free savings products available to UK tax payers subject to certain conditions and restrictions

Pension

People are living longer and choosing to retire earlier or work part-time. So, ensuring an adequate income from a pension has become more important. You need to find out from your employer what the pension arrangements are and what you can expect at your chosen retirement date, or find the information out yourself if you have invested in a personal pension scheme.

Insurance

Basic car insurance is compulsory, but otherwise insurance is generally a matter of personal choice. Complete the following schedule to record your insurance cover.

If you are unsure as to the cost of rebuilding your home or replacing your personal possessions, you should contact your insurance company and obtain their leaflets or website information which will guide you to calculate the amounts.

INSURANCE COVER

Date ______________________________

	Insurance Cover £	Replacement Cost £	Premium £
POSSESSIONS			
House Buildings			
Home Contents			
Jewellery			
Other Valuables			
Freezer Contents			
Car			
Income Protection			
Life Cover			
TOTAL			

Leisure and holidays

Holidays and leisure activities are an investment in your health. People who are too busy to take their full entitlement of holiday, and to find time to pursue leisure activities, are failing to achieve a sensible balance in their lifestyle and may be putting their health at risk. If you feel that you are too busy to make full use of holidays and leisure activities, you need to record what time you are devoting to these important activities.

Ask yourself and record:

- do you take your full holiday entitlement? If not, how much do you take?
- do you really manage to relax on holiday and return refreshed?
- how many evenings a week do you spend on leisure activities?
- how much time at weekends do you devote to leisure?

Appearance and image

Appearance and image have a significant influence on your life, for better or for worse. People instinctively pigeonhole us on appearance and speaking voice, and are likely to react and treat us accordingly. Currently – fortunately – things are less formal. What we are writing about here is not to preach conformism, but to get you to ask yourself what image you are projecting and to decide in fact, that it is the image that you are after.

Dress

Ask yourself and record:

- is your appearance in keeping with your job and the people internally and externally you deal with?
- do you know how to dress to suit the occasion, at work and/or in social settings?
- how often does your appearance attract favourable or unfavourable comment?

Grooming

Undoubtedly, grooming means different things to different people – hair, shoes, general state of clothes etc, but people do recognise good grooming or the lack of it. Good grooming singles people out, and gets them noticed in a favourable light both at work and socially.

Speaking voice

Research studies have shown that the qualities of a speaking voice have a dramatically greater effect, for better or for worse, than what is said. Accent is, of itself, not of great significance.

Ask yourself, and better still ask close family, friends and colleagues, and record:

- do you waffle, are long winded or ramble?
- do you modulate your voice or is it monotonous?
- is your speech unduly cliché ridden?
- how clear and precise is your diction?
- overall, is your speech an asset or a disadvantage?

Habits

Frequent habits can be irritating and give an impression of stress and anxiety. For example, scratching, nail chewing and finger tapping come into this category.

Ask yourself and record:

- do you have any irritating habits which attract comment or annoy someone either at work or at home?

APPEARANCE AND IMAGE

Date ____

Dress

Grooming

Speaking voice

Habits

Mental attitudes

Mental attitudes can, and often do, have a huge impact on people's lives and not necessarily for the better. Knowing yourself is vital for personal contentment, happiness and success. Some people know themselves extremely well early on in life and benefit accordingly, while others stumble through life never knowing themselves and suffer frustration and unhappiness.

Self-esteem

Self-esteem is the key mental attitude. The evidence is that people with a high self-esteem will achieve more and be better fulfilled than those with a low self-esteem.

Ask yourself and record:

- what are the characteristics, traits and skills you have which you are pleased about, and dissatisfied with?

Other mental attitudes

If you really want to change your life, then the starting point is to change some of your mental attitudes and this means you have to face up to reality.

Ask yourself and record:

- have you a burning ambition and hunger to be rich, successful or famous?
- are you prepared to devote yourself entirely to achieve this?
- how happy are you, and what would make you happier?
- how lonely are you, and what would markedly improve your situation?
- do you have fears or phobias which affect your everyday life?

MENTAL ATTITUDES

Date ______________________________

Self-esteem

Ambition

Happiness

Loneliness

Fears and phobias

Qualifications, skills and personal development

Formal qualifications help, but in no way guarantee either success or happiness. There are plenty of entrepreneurs, executives, writers, journalists, musicians, artists and chefs who've achieved spectacular success without formal qualifications. Some were hopeless at school, others turned their back on further education or dropped out of their course. Whilst professional success in law, medicine, accountancy and similar careers requires formal qualifications, the rest of the working world does not. In many walks of life your natural ability, skills you have developed, enthusiasm and personality will take you as far as you wish to go.

Record:

- your formal qualifications
- job related training which is transferable, e.g. using specific software packages, sales skills, recruitment interviewing
- natural abilities which you do not utilise fully, e.g. creative writing, painting, technical drawing, cooking
- leisure activities which could provide a new career or self employment, e.g. gardening, designing and making clothes
- what personal development have you done recently or are doing currently?

QUALIFICATIONS, SKILLS AND PERSONAL DEVELOPMENT

Date ______________________________

Formal qualifications

Transferable work skills

Natural abilities

Leisure activities

Personal development

Direction and goals

Having goals and a set direction are neither a prerequisite for success, happiness and contentment, nor a guarantee of it. Indeed, some people stumble across the very thing which brings them what they want from life in abundance. The inescapable truth is, however, that having goals and a direction dramatically increases the likelihood of success, happiness and contentment for most people.

Some people have decided their direction in life, and even their goals, before becoming a teenager. This may or may not be a good thing, but it is likely to shape the rest of their life. Harold Wilson was photographed as a child standing on the steps of 10 Downing Street, and the fact that he became Prime Minister was not mere coincidence.

Equally, the likelihood of young people pursuing a career for life is becoming increasingly improbable and many would rightly reject the concept as unappealing and unrealistic. Working lives are likely to be a series of episodes, during which it is important to develop transferable skills and to open up a wide range of work and career opportunities for the future. The pace of change will accelerate, fuelled by technological development – valuable skills will become redundant and new ones will need to be learned.

Use the space which follows to record your goals and direction. If you do not have any conscious goals or direction, then simply leave the page blank. Categorically, this is no cause for concern, self criticism nor does it indicate a lack of imagination. Don't worry about setting goals for yourself, because the next chapter is expressly designed to help you to do this.

EXISTING GOALS AND DIRECTION

Date ______________________________

CHAPTER

02

TAKE CONTROL OF YOUR LIFE: SET YOUR OWN GOALS (WHOSE LIFE IS IT ANYWAY?)

02

'A person's reach should exceed their grasp'

Anon

Simply writing your goals down on paper is merely the first step in what may prove a long and arduous journey to make them become a reality, but it is the vital first step. An essential ingredient is personal belief that you will achieve your goals. So you need to convince yourself, and marshal the tangible evidence, that you can and will achieve your goals. Constantly reminding yourself of your goals and thinking about them, encourages your subconscious mind to take over and accelerate your achievement. Mental rehearsal of success is important as well. Picture in your mind's eye, over and over again, what it will feel like when you have achieved your goals.

Is there any evidence that these techniques work, or is it merely hocus pocus? Yes, they work! Some years ago behavioural scientists took 30 volunteers, divided them into two groups randomly. Each group was asked to play darts and the average scores were recorded. One group was asked to practise each day for three weeks. The other group was asked not to practise at all, but to mentally rehearse the darts landing where they aimed, and three weeks later they completely outperformed the people who practised. This is merely one of countless controlled experiments.

Goals come with a price tag attached. Part of the price tag may involve incurring some expenses, such as tuition costs to gain an extra qualification. Usually, however, the onerous part of the price tag is the time, effort and single mindedness required to achieve the goal. This means that you need to recognise the price tag attached to a goal, and be totally prepared to pay it in full, before you decide to set yourself that goal.

Goals need to be measurable, not subjective or elastic. If your weight loss goal is to lose three kilos within the next three months, then whether or not you have achieved it, or how nearly so, is measurable. If your goal is merely to lose some weight over the next few months, then it comes complete with ample scope to make excuses or to rationalise that your performance wasn't too bad in the circumstances.

Timescales are important for successfully achieving goals. If you have a goal to accumulate a share portfolio worth more than £1 million within a ten year period, it is vitally important to have sub-goals for what progress you will have achieved in, say, three months, and in one, three and five years. So, the statement of your goals which you are asked to fill in at the end of this chapter is classified both by individual goals and by timescales.

When setting goals for yourself, comprehensiveness has no merit. Whilst the questionnaire is comprehensive, you are urged only to set goals for the things you really want and are committed to achieve, believe you will achieve and are determined to do so. It is much more productive to set only one or two short-term goals, and to achieve them, and be inspired to set new goals, than to set numerous goals only to give up in despair.

Work and career

Your goal may be as immediate as to ask the boss for a pay rise. Alternatively, it could be to gain promotion within your own department or elsewhere in the company. Equally, your goal could be to be trained within the company to change your career from, say, customer support engineer to technical sales. Other possibilities may be to be relocated at home or overseas either to improve the overall quality of your life or to gain international experience. The stress, pressures, internal politics or culture of your employer may be such that you should leave as soon as possible either to find similar work elsewhere or to find completely different work even though it may be less well paid.

Starting your own business

Perhaps your dream is to start your own company, to be self-employed or to turn a hobby into an income. Dreams can and do become a reality, but serendipity or sitting back and waiting for it to happen are not recommended. A sensible short-term goal would be to identify an opportunity, research the marketplace and to develop a sound business plan in your spare time before deciding to leave your present job.

Health

It is so easy and commonplace to take health for granted, and only realise the fundamental importance of good health when faced with serious illness. All the success and wealth in the world count for very little without good health. So health improvement should be a series of continuing goals for everyone throughout life, starting now.

There is so much scope for health improvement, that everyone should set at least one goal. Pick the single thing which could be most beneficial for your health and set yourself an achievable goal for the next three months, but a measurable one so that you cannot deceive yourself or make excuses. Refer back to the Health questionnaire which you completed earlier, to help you decide which goal(s) to set. Apps on your phone can prove useful.

Relevant goals you could set include:

- to limit your weekly alcohol intake to a particular number of units, and to record how much you drink to avoid deceiving yourself
- to join a gym club or an exercise class and attend twice a week
- use an exercise DVD or an online 'course'' twice a week
- to take a brisk 30 minute walk every lunchtime
- to stop eating biscuits, cake and crisps for three months
- to eat some fruit and salad every day

Appearance and image

Improved grooming and eliminating irritating personal habits do not require you to spend more than a little money. It boils down to developing routines which work for you, not against you (eg washing your hair regularly, shoes kept well repaired and cleaned, nails should be tidily cut and impeccably clean). Irritating habits identified in your Appearance and Image questionnaire (completed earlier) should be eliminated. Decide what your objectives are to be, and write them down.

Dress matters. You should consider clothes and appearance as an investment and not an expense. Style, taste, colour combinations and accessories are important. Decide how much you can afford to invest and set yourself priorities. Visit up-market clothes stores or search the web for ideas and advice, even if you don't buy there, and read style magazines. Consider using a personal shopper to help you choose clothes. Some departmental stores offer this service free. A carefully chosen and good quality accessory can enhance cheaper clothes, but a visibly cheap accessory or a well-worn one will detract from good clothes. At work a cheap ballpoint pen, a tattered briefcase or bag and a silly 'fun' watch can create a negative effect.

Self development – qualifications, skills and personal development

Obtaining qualifications, learning new skills and pursuing personal development takes time and energy, which probably means less time available for family, friends and leisure pursuits. Before deciding what goals to set yourself, find out what support is available from your employer. Some employers offer day release, internal and external short courses and some pay for attending evening classes or distance learning on completion of the course. Even if your employer does not appear to offer much, why not ask? What have you got to lose? If your goal is to complete an MBA from Harvard Business School, why not ask your employer if they would consider providing some financial support.

If the opportunities you want are not available during working hours and provided by your employer, think carefully before setting your goals. Ask yourself do you have the time, energy and determination to complete the course? What else will suffer in your life? Why are you thinking of pursuing this course? If it is for career advancement and increased earning power, what tangible evidence is available to demonstrate that it will be worthwhile?

Relationships

Spectacular success and substantial financial wealth may bring little happiness or comfort by themselves. Meaningful relationships with your partner, children, parents, friends and work colleagues will bring enjoyment and happiness. There is a snag, however. Meaningful relationships require investing time, not just to build in the first place, but to sustain as well. Inevitably relationships suffer or fail because people have insufficient time, or more accurately because they do not make enough time. So, it may be necessary to choose a single type of relationship on which to devote more time.

Networking

Networking might seem an irrelevant goal to focus on, but networking can dramatically enhance and accelerate achieving your other goals. If you wish, you can simply dismiss networking as using the old school tie or exploiting the people you know. Effective networking is entirely different. It is not simply about exchanging contact details with people whom you happen to meet and compiling a database.

Effective networking should commence by deciding which networks could best help you achieve your goals. For example, most companies are members of their trade or industry association. You could visit the association's website to find out about conferences, seminars, discussion forums, regional and national dinners. Try an event and assess the networking potential. If you have a professional qualification, find out about industry sector groups and working parties which could provide networking opportunities. Business school alumni groups, software users clubs and suchlike organisations provide countless opportunities if you think about it. Search and use online networking sites like LinkedIn.

Effective networking requires more than meeting people who may help you to achieve your goals, it requires building and maintaining contact and developing a constructive rapport and relationship with interesting and worthwhile people.

Personal reinvention

Personal reinvention is achievable, but you may ask what does it mean? Generally speaking, personal reinvention means achieving a dramatic change in your lifestyle. By its very nature it may have to be a medium or long-term goal because of everything that has to be put in place to make it possible, but there is no way that reinvention should be dismissed as impossible or even relegated to a distant pipe dream.

Before you conclude that personal reinvention is definitely not for you, please consider some examples. Whether or not these particular examples strike any chord with you is irrelevant, but they may just inspire you to decide that some other form of personal reinvention would suit you down to the ground:

- transform a hobby into a full-time occupation which provides an acceptable income, e.g. woodcarving
- make a major career change in midlife, e.g. qualify as a solicitor or a modern languages teacher
- exchange urban living for a simple rural lifestyle or escape to a remote island
- set a target date, even if it's 10 or 15 years away, to have retired from traditional employment (there is plenty of time to decide what you will do instead)
- give up your career and become a 'househusband' or 'housewife' while your partner concentrates on a full-time career
- take a one year sabbatical from your career to write your first novel

These examples are not hypothetical, each one was pursued by an acquaintance of the authors.

Leisure

If you thoroughly enjoy spending all of your spare time as a couch potato watching television or playing computer games (even though you are 35 and married), so be it. The whole point about setting goals, however, is that you have an opportunity to make choices which could enhance your career, earning power, relationships, health or personal fulfillment and development. Consider some of the choices open to you:

- learn a language
- return to a sport or take up a new one
- join a special interest club
- develop a new skill
- start a business part-time which you would really enjoy

PERSONAL GOALS

Date ____________________

	3 months	12 months
Work and career		
Health		
Appearance and image		
Personal development		
Relationships		
Networking		
Personal reinvention		
Leisure		

3 years	5 years	Long-term

CHAPTER

03

MANAGE YOUR FINANCES AND CREATE PERSONAL WEALTH

03

You do not need to be either a qualified accountant or a financial expert to manage your finances better and to create wealth for you and your family. This chapter will equip you to do both.

Personal income and expenditure

Refer back to the Estimated Income and Expenditure Statement you completed earlier. If your total annual income exceeds your total expenditure then you have a sound basis for beginning to create wealth and if income and expenditure are roughly equal then it is a satisfactory state of affairs. When expenditure exceeds income then you are living beyond your means and you need to identify which items of discretionary expenditure you can reduce or eliminate to avoid becoming deeper in debt. If your essential expenditure exceeds your total income then prompt action is needed. If it is a temporary state of affairs, perhaps because you are unemployed at present, then a solution could be to arrange an authorised overdraft from your bank or borrow some money from a relative.

If you simply cannot meet your essential expenditure on a continuing basis, then urgent action must be taken. Despair or resignation offer no way out. You need to visit both the Citizens Advice Bureau and the Department of Social Security to make sure you are receiving all the regular housing and income benefits you are entitled to. This may still leave you facing an income shortfall and it may be necessary to actively seek part-time employment which fits in with responsibilities for caring for your children or aged relatives.

It has to be recognised that resorting to money lenders or loan sharks will inevitably make matters worse. Beware, too, of loan consolidators which convert your various debts into a new loan arrangement. Read the small print carefully, the initial charges may be sizeable and there may be substantial risks and penalties for failing to maintain regular repayments. Similarly, spending money on gambling, whether it be horse racing or lottery tickets must be rejected. Every effort must be made to get out of the vicious circle of deepening debt.

Borrowing and debt

Refer back to the Borrowing and Debt schedule you completed earlier. The key to effective personal debt management is simplicity, because the more sources of debt you have the more difficult it is to manage.

Some financial institutions offer a single account which combines a mortgage loan and a bank account with a drawing facility. You will be better off regardless of whether your bank account is usually in surplus or overdrawn. For example, consider a separate mortgage of, say, £60,000 with an interest rate of 3 per cent. and a £2,000 overdraft with interest of 12 per cent. If this is reorganised into a single loan account of £62,000 at an interest rate of 3 per cent., then there will be a saving of £180 a year before taking into account income tax. If your current account is always in surplus, the interest you receive will inevitably be less than the interest rate on your mortgage, so you will be better off.

The most effective use of credit cards is always to pay the outstanding balance in full by the date when interest is charged and ideally you would authorise the credit card company to collect the payment by direct debit so that you never pay a monthly interest charge simply because you forgot to post a cheque in time. In this way, you enjoy up to five or six weeks interest free credit permanently on your credit card expenditure.

The reality may be, however, that you simply do not have sufficient available cash to pay off the outstanding sums you owe on credit cards. Nonetheless there is action you can take to reduce the amount of interest you pay because credit card companies may charge nearly 20 per cent. APR (annualised percentage rate) and store credit cards may cost nearly 30 per cent. APR. Possible courses of action are:

- if you have a combined mortgage and current account, explore the possibility of using this account to pay off all your credit card balances because the interest rate will be substantially lower.
- visit financial advice websites or read personal finance supplements of newspapers, often published at weekends, reporting or advertising credit card companies and internet bank credit cards offering a bargain interest rate for the first six months on balances transferred from other credit cards.
- take out an authorised overdraft facility on your current account or arrange a personal loan with monthly repayments, at a lower interest cost, to pay off your credit card balances.

Another interest saving opportunity is to replace an unauthorised overdraft by an authorised one. When you don't have an authorised overdraft facility there is every likelihood that your bank will delight in charging you both a fixed fee and a hefty interest charge every time your current account dips into the red even if only for a day. In contrast, an authorised overdraft facility should avoid the fixed fee charged for being overdrawn and incur a lower rate of interest.

A property mortgage – and there are different types – offers the possibility of a sizeable interest saving. The first step is to establish what percentage APR you are paying, the notice period and any termination costs you face for prematurely switching to another mortgage provider. Even if you have to pay a termination charge, it is possible that either another mortgage provider will reimburse you in order to win your business or that the lower interest rate you can obtain will quickly exceed the termination charge.

A decision to switch your mortgage should not be taken hastily. Visit websites and read personal financial supplements to find articles about mortgages. Take note of any financial advisers or mortgage providers written about by journalists. It is a fair bet, but not a guarantee, that they have done some homework to ensure that they are only naming reputable advisers and mortgage providers.

There is a good case for contacting two or three financial advisers to find out what kind of mortgage they recommend and which mortgage providers. Do ask them how much commission they will receive from each product they recommend, and ask if they are prepared to rebate some of their commission to you, so that you find out if they are making recommendations which maximise their income. Also, recognise that contacting a financial adviser does not oblige you to do business with them, you can still shop around by making direct contact with mortgage providers yourself.

Do not be seduced by special offers. Some companies offer a low and fixed percentage APR for, say, two years and a variable rate afterwards. It is essential that you understand the basis on which the variable rate will be set and whether or not you will end up paying more interest. Similarly, you must find out your freedom to switch mortgage provider in the future and the termination costs involved.

Savings

You should take opportunities to make savings by spending, provided that the time and expense involved really do add up to a worthwhile saving. Some credit cards offer a 1 per cent. discount on all purchases up to about £20,000 a year, and may give up to 4 per cent. discount from certain suppliers such as theatre ticket agencies. Provided you always avoid paying interest charges on your credit card, then the discount offers a genuine and effortless saving. If you are in the habit of paying interest on outstanding balances, then it is essential to check that any discount is not outweighed by higher interest charges.

Several major banks pay little or no amount of gross interest, before deduction of income tax, on current account credit balances. In sharp contrast, some internet banks and traditional building societies offer current accounts with a gross interest rate well above the rate of inflation. Alternatively, transfer genuinely surplus cash from your current account to a separate deposit account which pays a competitive rate of interest.

Your basic savings objective should be to build up a 'rainy day fund' in an instant access deposit account, paying a decent interest rate, to cope with unexpected expenses such as household or car repairs, without having to resort to an expensive overdraft.

If you have more money on deposit than needed to cope with rainy day expenses, then options to be considered include:

- switching surplus cash to a notice period deposit account, which requires from 30 to 180 days notice to make a withdrawal to avoid incurring a penalty for early withdrawal. The extra interest to be earned could be up to another 2 per cent. per annum depending upon the length of notice period accepted.

- finding out what tax free interest rates are available on deposits with government agencies such as National Savings Certificates in the UK. Typically, the deposit periods are fixed for two, three or five year periods and early withdrawal results in substantially lower and generally uncompetitive rates of interest.

The stark reality of savings deposits during the past 25 years, however, is that even the best interest rates, after deducting the standard rate of income tax payable, have barely exceeded the level of inflation. So it must be clearly understood that savings deposits really only protect your capital against inflation and do not create increased wealth for you.

In recent years bank account interest rates have been at historic lows. Despite this, governments do offer tax free savings opportunities from time to time which should be regarded as the core of a savings plan. In the UK, an Individual Savings Account (Cash ISA) for example, allows up to £20,000 a year to be saved tax free.

For wealthy people with sizeable savings in the UK, Premium Savings Bonds should not be overlooked. The tax free interest rate is usually above the level of inflation. The maximum holding for an individual is £50,000 and whilst the odds of a single £1 bond winning a prize is about 34,500 to 1 against every month, a fairly reliable income can be expected from the maximum holding permitted, and there is always the possibility of winning one of the prizes ranging from £25 to £1 million in each monthly draw.

Investments

The essence of investment is the prospect of achieving a higher rate of return than can be earned from interest payable on a deposit account, with the attendant risk of losing some or all of the capital invested. There is a golden rule about investment schemes which you should follow religiously, and for that matter it applies equally to savings schemes: if the rewards offered seem too good to be true then the 'scheme' is probably too good to be true and should be avoided at all costs.

Thousands of people in the UK invested heavily in an off-shore deposit scheme producing returns of up to 18 per cent. per annum from gilt-edged securities, when the market rate of return was only about a third of this, and lost their capital. Countless people have invested in foreign ostrich farms, without even confirming the farm existed, seduced by the promise of spectacular returns at no risk and ended up with nothing. So stay clear of the next bizarre scheme promising to make you rich and guaranteed to be risk free.

Home ownership, using a mortgage, should be your first investment priority. Whilst property prices have fallen at times during the past 50 years in the UK, the overwhelming majority of people have increased their personal capital from home ownership in real terms. Also, of course, it brings the dividend of the pleasure of home ownership as well. If you aren't yet a homeowner, your priority should be to buy your first home as soon as possible and start climbing the home ownership ladder. Otherwise, if property prices rise faster than inflation, it becomes progressively harder to be able to pay the monthly mortgage installments. The first step should be to find out:

- the size of the mortgage that your monthly property rental costs would support

- if you are able to afford a larger monthly mortgage payment than your present rental costs, how large a mortgage could you obtain.

The next stage in your investment plan should be to invest in the ordinary shares of stockmarket listed companies. Since the end of the Second World War, the return from quoted shares has handsomely outperformed deposit interest and provided opportunities for individuals to create wealth for themselves. In any one year, however, share prices may fall significantly across the whole stockmarket of a particular country or even worldwide, so it is entirely possible to lose some capital in the short-term. Individual shares perform even more erratically. Some blue chip share prices do fall by more than 50 per cent. in a year, and some listed companies end up in receivership. In the dot-com bubble, companies enjoyed rocketing share prices for several months, and then many suffered drastic price falls or failure.

Two key messages should be apparent in order to reduce the risk. Stockmarket investments should be made with at least a five year timescale in mind. Avoid investing money which you will need to realise in, say, a year's time because you may be obliged to sell at a low point, incur a hefty loss and be unable to wait for an inevitable upturn. Secondly, spreading your investment rather than gambling everything on one company can substantially reduce the risk of loss.

In the UK, people are allowed to invest up to a total of £20,000 each fiscal year in an Individual Savings Account (ISA) and the whole amount may be invested in shares. Both dividends, which are accumulated, and capital gains are tax free.

To spread the risk, you can invest in a wide range of unit trusts and investment trusts, which invest across a range of companies, and are managed by specialist fund managers. It is important to understand the difference between a unit trust and an investment trust. The value of a unit trust moves up or down directly as a result of the movement in the shares invested in. Investors are usually charged an introductory commission on purchasing units, which can be up to about 5 per cent. of the amount invested. Discount brokers who advertise in personal finance supplements of newspapers and via their website offer substantial savings by rebating the bulk of the introductory commission. In addition to this commission the fund manager will charge an annual management fee in the region of 1 per cent. to 1.5 per cent.

Investment trusts are quite different in structure. Each one is a listed company on a stockmarket, and it may well have the power to borrow money in order to maximise the return for investors. So the share price of the investment trust does not rise or fall in direct proportion to the value of the underlying share investments. Also, the share price of the investment trust can increase or fall depending upon the number of people buying or selling the shares. Although the buying and selling costs for investment trusts, and the management fees as well, are lower than for unit trusts, they are more complex and often more volatile so initially investors should stick with unit trusts.

Unit trusts, and investment trusts as well, are marketed as either general or specialist funds. So it is important to understand the different degree of risk involved. As a broad generalisation, income trusts which are invested in substantial companies primarily for their dividend income prospects will be low risk. Whereas a specialist fund investing only in fledgling biotech companies will be high risk. Similarly, many funds which invest solely in one emerging market country, say, Thailand, will involve greater risk than a global emerging market fund which may invest across 30 or more countries.

Clearly, the potential gain and loss from investing in individual shares is greater. Statistically, however, a portfolio invested in a dozen different companies would involve significantly lower risk, and there would be less risk still if the investments were spread across various business sectors. Numerous online share dealing companies offer fixed price dealing costs, which are substantially lower than the charges of traditional stockbrokers which may charge more than 1.5 per cent. of the value of shares bought or sold.

If you are tempted to buy and sell shares yourself, it is important to understand the difference between the bid and offer price. For a leading company, the purchase (offer) price may be 300p and the sale (bid) price may be 297p, in other words a sale automatically costs 1 per cent., because of the price spread, plus the dealing costs of buying and selling the shares. For much smaller companies, where shares are bought and sold infrequently and usually only in small quantities, the spread may well be 5 per cent. and at times could reach 10 per cent. So there must be a significant gain in the share price before the investor makes any profit.

Various systems have been used to limit losses. One is the 'stop loss' approach. Whenever a share falls by, say, 10 per cent. or 15 per cent. below either the purchase price or a higher market price reached subsequently, it is automatically sold. Some people combine the 'stop loss' with a 'lock in gains' approach. When a share rises by 50 per cent., half of the holding will be sold arbitrarily, and when the share price reaches double the purchase cost then 50 per cent. of the remaining shares will be sold, and so on.

An enjoyable and low cost way of dealing in shares is to join an investment club. A standard set of rules signed by each member is essential. Typically, a club will have between 10 and 20 members, each person will invest a minimum of perhaps £50 to £100 each month, members will meet monthly to discuss buying and selling opportunities, and an elected committee will make investment decisions on behalf of all the members.

For people with £50,000 or more to invest in shares, plenty of fund managers will manage a portfolio of unit trusts to achieve a given capital growth and risk profile. For amounts usually in excess of £500,000, fund managers will manage a tailored portfolio of unit trusts, investment trusts and individual shares. These services usually provide full discretion to the fund manager, and the client receives a quarterly valuation report and an annual statement of capital gains and losses, and dividend income for tax purposes. The cost of these services is about 1 per cent. of the total sum invested, plus the cost of buying and selling shares for the portfolio.

Clearly, there are many other forms of investment available. Venture capital trusts or Enterprise Investment Schemes invest in a range of unquoted companies, and have valuable tax benefits. These should be regarded as higher risk investments and would normally be restricted to a small percentage of a large investment portfolio. Other investments include commercial or residential property for letting, art, wine and collectibles. When making investments like these a key assessment to make is how easily realisable the investment may be at times when the market is depressed.

An effective means of building capital is by investing a fixed sum each month in a unit or investment trust, usually payable by direct debit. Most schemes accept sums from as little as £50 per month. One benefit of this approach is that the risk of investing a lump sum near a high point in the price is avoided. Also, when the price falls the fixed monthly investment purchases more shares as shown by the following table:

Month	**Investment**	**Share Price**	**Number of Shares**
January	£100	100p	100
February	£100	80p	125
March	£100	66.7p	150
April	**£100**	100p	**100**
TOTAL COST	**£400**		**475**

So after four monthly investments, although the share price has not increased a total of 475 shares have been bought with a current market value of £475, showing a profit of £75 or 17.5 per cent.

Pensions

Pensions are boring to the young and a matter of real importance as you grow older. Basic state pensions are an inadequate source of income even to cover basic living costs, yet many people are forced to retire by age 50, or want to, and they need an income for the next 30 years or more. Regular pension investment needs to start in your twenties, in order to provide a decent pension. For example, taking into account the state pension of £144 a week (under the new single-tier state pension rules), an individual would have to save £1,000 a month from the age of 30 to 66 in order to top up their state pension to £25,000 a year or £2,100 a month.

A rule of thumb as to the amount you should save is to take your current income and remove the last two digits, and that's the amount you should pay into your pension each month. So, for example, if you earn £25,000 a year, you should be paying £250 into your pension each month.

A workplace pension scheme (and auto-enrolment) helps those in employment, but the self-employed need to take action too. To be adequately pensioned you need to invest at least 15% of your annual salary from age 25 onwards!

Insurance

The purposes of insurance is to protect your assets, your income and lifestyle, and your dependents in the event of your untimely death.

If your home and the contents are either not insured or inadequately so, you are taking a risk which could damage your assets and your lifestyle. A priority should be to ensure that your home and contents are fully insured.

Life insurance may well be one of the benefits provided by your employer. A sum of four times your annual basic salary is common-place, and your dependents will normally receive it tax free. If you are self-employed, however, there is a strong case for arranging your own life insurance cover to ensure your dependents are provided for adequately.

Income protection against illness is often provided by employers, and a typical benefit would be 50 per cent. of your basic salary payable after either three or six months of continuous absence. Once again, if you are self-employed you should arrange your own insurance.

Wills

There is a strong argument for every adult having a properly prepared and witnessed Will, which should be reviewed and amended as necessary, say, every five years to reflect changes in your wishes, circumstances and legislation. Without a Will, there are rigid guidelines which determine the allocation of your estate, which may be very different from your wishes, and there could be delay in distributing the proceeds of your Will.

Inheritance Tax is payable in the UK on all estates in excess of about £325,000 at 40 per cent. Given the high level of house prices, many people face the prospect of paying Inheritance Tax. This liability can be eliminated or reduced by a combination of timely gifts and the creation of trusts. You should guesstimate the value of your personal wealth, and if you face a sizeable Inheritance Tax liability, professional advice should be taken and arrangements incorporated into your Will.

Effective personal financial management and wealth creation require a written action plan. A worked example is shown below, followed by a blank version for you to complete.

Put a value on yourself

In all this, it is easy to underestimate the value of yourself in terms of what might be called your own capital worth in your ability to generate earned income.

For example, it is easy to understand that if you were to have unearned income (say bank interest) of £30,000, then at a generous interest rate of 2 per cent, you would have capital in the bank of £1.5million.

But, if you earn £30,000, why not say to yourself: "Hey! I'm worth £1.5million", for that is the amount you would need to have in savings in order to generate that return.

Yes, we know that you are working for your salary, but that does not mean you can forget that you are yourself a capital asset – so, look after yourself and develop the asset and make it produce even more of a return.

PERSONAL FINANCIAL MANAGEMENT AND WEALTH CREATION ACTION PLAN

Date ____

	Action	**Deadline**
Mortgage	Check freedom and cost of switching mortgage. Find out about available mortgage types. Arrange a new mortgage.	End January End January End March
Overdraft	Convert the unauthorised overdraft to an authorised one sufficient to pay off credit card balances.	Mid January
Credit cards	Pay off credit card balances.	Mid February
Other loan	-	
Savings Accounts	Check the current rate of interest on the £250 balance in an old building society account.	End January
Cash ISAs	Plan to invest some money during the fiscal year commencing 6 April.	April onwards
National Savings Certificates		
Premium Bonds		
Equity ISAs	Select a low risk unit trust and invest £50 per month by direct debit.	From April

	Action	Deadline
Unit Trusts	-	
Investment Trusts	-	
Shares	-	
Other investments	-	
Pensions	Get my employer/pension provider to calculate my likely pension income at either age 50 or 60.	February
Home and contents insurance	Estimate the rebuilding cost of our home and the replacement value of the contents and increase the sum insured.	End February
Life insurance	Check what benefit my employer offers.	Next week
Income protection	Check what benefit my employer offers.	Next week
Wills	Visit a solicitor and have a Will written.	Easter

PERSONAL FINANCIAL MANAGEMENT AND WEALTH CREATION ACTION PLAN

Date ______________________________

Date	Action	Deadline

PERSONAL FINANCIAL MANAGEMENT AND WEALTH CREATION ACTION PLAN

Date ____________________

Date	Action	Deadline

CHAPTER 04

PERSONAL SKILLS

04

Introduction

Human skills, intuition and wisdom are replacing capital as the most precious corporate resource. You should ensure that you develop portable skills that go wherever you go, whether in employment or self-employment. You should develop your skills and know-how in relevant technical subjects that interest you and which will be of value and in general management skills and practices. You should constantly polish your product and hone your skills in, for example, time management, creative thinking, decision making, problem solving as well as general communication skills. Undertake reading or training in and around your current job to develop skills you need for the next stage in your career. Don't wait to be trained and prompted – make yourself the automatic choice. You can, and the best people do, define their own job progression and you can do this best by acquiring and using those skills that people and businesses need most.

For most people in the early years of work, the prospect of a career for life or spending a lifetime with one employer is improbable, and many people would regard it as totally unappealing anyway. Careers are likely to be a series of episodes, working for very different kinds of organisations, with the real prospect of wanting to be self-employed at some stage or to start your own company. In their forties, more and more people want to have control of their lives and may choose a combination of part-time work, self employment, charity work and more time spent pursuing a hobby.

The curriculum vitae is not dead or irrelevant yet, because there is no substitute for tangible achievement, but it will become increasingly important to develop portable, exploitable and enduring skills throughout your whole working life. Inevitably, information technology, the Internet, mobile communications and e-commerce will devalue skills and expertise which were valued by employers only a few years earlier.

An attractive CV might include:

- employment experience
  - with a multinational company
  - with an overseas company
  - with a start-up business
  - with a competitor company
- education
  - degree
  - postgraduate qualification(s)
- interests
  - sports
  - charity work
  - travel
- skills training
  - finance
  - technology
  - management and leadership
  - presentation
  - marketing
  - project management.

Technology

Information technology in the widest sense is the bandwagon you must be aboard and remain so. If you are under 40, the likelihood is that you have developed your computer/tablet/smartphone skills throughout your working life.

If you are not completely computer literate, urgent action is needed now. There are a number of options open to you, such as:

- ask your children (yes, your children), partner, relative or friend to give you some basic training and understanding
- buy your own personal computer, laptop, tablet or smart-phone so that you can experiment and learn in private, if this is your preference
- if your understanding is adequate but your keyboard skills are slow, take every opportunity to practice at work and home
- if you find instruction manuals daunting, search online to find a personal coach. It will not merely be money well spent, it will be an invaluable investment for the rest of your life
- if you cannot afford personal tuition, consider joining a local evening class for beginners or improvers
- ask a colleague or assistant at work to give you some personal tuition, if necessary during the lunchbreak or after office hours
- ask your employer to send you on a training course or, better still, arrange some personal tuition provided by the information technology department or the external IT services provider or local computer stores.

Hopefully, nowadays very few people whose work benefits from information technology literacy will not have the requisite skills. So the priority should be to develop your skills and keep abreast of relevant technological advances. To achieve this your choice of employer is important. The company you have chosen to work for should be totally committed to using and developing the latest information technology tools. In this way, you have the opportunity to learn new techniques continuously and, equally important, information technology and knowledge management are so fundamental to corporate success, so the company should be able to deliver ample opportunities for promotion and wide experience. Technology is so important that if your employer is not really committed, then there is a strong case for finding another employer.

Your objective should be to gain recognition for your information technology skills. Opportunities to achieve this include:

- volunteer to be a guinea pig for testing new software tools and equipment
- join working parties involved with introducing upgraded or new technology, particularly when this will involve working with either internal IT specialists or external consultants so that you can learn from them
- consider joining a user group for a particular supplier's products or an industry user group
- visit websites and read technology magazines to find out about tools and equipment which could benefit your employer and to learn of training courses which could enhance your skills

Put it another way, your brain is your software – yes you have to keep the hardware (your physical condition) in proper working order, but as with computing, the real value is the constantly improving software. So take care of both elements.

Speaking skills

Your voice and speaking skills could have a significant impact on your career success, for better or for worse. People are all too ready, either consciously or subconsciously, to pigeonhole people on hearing them speak.

Your speaking voice can be improved. There are books and videos designed to help you speak more effectively. Toastmasters International is a worldwide non-profit making organisation designed to help people to speak effectively in public, which could be an audience of two people or several hundreds. There may well be a branch near you. There are an increasing number of voice coaches, advertising in local and national newspapers, who will provide one to one coaching if you feel reluctant to learn in a group, but group learning is often great fun as well and a way of making new friends.

Better still, your company may hold internal training courses or be prepared to pay for external training. The ability to speak effectively, with persuasion and impact, is equally important whether having an informal discussion with a colleague or addressing a conference. Find out about voice coaches for business and public training courses, do your homework and convince your employer to pay for you to develop your skills.

You may feel that you have little to learn or benefit from voice coaching or public speaking tuition. Most people are shocked to find out just how much improvement they did achieve. Effective speaking is not just about projection, pronunciation and modulation. Posture, body language, keeping mannerisms under control, word formatting for maximum interest and attention, and the use of pauses are some of the techniques which can be more important than the speaking voice itself.

Word formatting was developed by leading academics and is widely used by political leaders to express themselves with impact and appeal, but can work for everyone. For example, instead of saying to your department 'I want us all to work together on this project...', consider saying 'I cannot implement the project successfully by myself. The department managers are committed to the project and cannot complete it alone, but if we all pull together, I passionately believe it will be a great success and at the same time we can make our work more enjoyable.'

Financial knowledge

The key asset of any business is the human resources and knowledge base, but a common denominator is finance. For anyone who aspires to have overall responsibility for profit, whether it is a small business unit, a subsidiary company or a global group, financial knowledge is a prerequisite. You may get the job with the profit responsibility you really want despite your lack of financial knowledge, but by then it may be too late to learn what you need to know in order to succeed or even to manage to hang onto your job.

In the years ahead, your working life is likely to take directions which you never anticipated. More and more people will become self-employed or start a business and by then you must have the requisite financial knowledge.

Even if you are absolutely determined that you will never be responsible for profit or never become self-employed or never start your own business, you should still consider acquiring financial knowledge. When putting forward ideas and recommendations, you will be able to evaluate the financial impact and affordability to help sell your case. Also, financial knowledge is a fundamental business skill which is portable and enduring.

Test the extent and depth of your financial knowledge by completing the following questionnaire.

FINANCIAL KNOWLEDGE QUESTIONNAIRE

Date ______________________________

Can you personally or do you: **√ or X each box**

1. Read and understand a profit and loss account? ☐
2. Read and understand every item on a balance sheet? ☐
3. Produce a profit and loss and cash flow budget? ☐
4. Restate a profit and loss account to show the variable costs, marginal profit (amount and percentage), fixed overheads and profit? ☐
5. Calculate a breakeven point for your business? ☐
6. Understand the constituents of working capital and know how to manage them? ☐
7. Understand discounted cash flow techniques used for evaluating investment decisions? ☐

Unless you have scored 100 per cent., you need to improve your financial skills. You have no excuses, because there are ample opportunities to learn. Online learning is available, companies organise in-house courses and many training companies and professional bodies present training courses.

Industry sector knowledge

Admittedly if you move out of your present industry sector, and it is more likely to be when rather than if, then this knowledge will become redundant overnight. This does not diminish the importance of actively acquiring sector knowledge, even if you could well only spend two or three years working in the sector.

You will benefit in a variety of ways, including:

- learning about technological developments which could provide opportunities or threats for your business and your career
- becoming aware of new tools and software
- finding out about takeovers and mergers which could pose a competitive threat or affect your customer or supplier base
- getting early warning of legislative or regulatory issues which could affect your business or provide new opportunities
- spotting new business opportunities
- becoming recognised within your own company as a sector expert
- finding out about potential new employers and career opportunities.

If you take your career seriously, regardless of the particular job you do, become knowledgeable about your sector. Find out which websites and trade press are most relevant for you, and keep informed.

Time management skills

For most people, 20 per cent. of their working time produces 80 per cent. of their contribution for the company. Yet many people are so busy 'working' unthinkingly and indiscriminately, that they simply do not make time to do the 20 per cent. which would produce 80 per cent. of their effectiveness.

Information technology is designed to make people more productive, yet some people manage to become less efficient. Consider the internal email; some people boast about receiving 50 or even 100 every day and meticulously read every one even though many of them are irrelevant, and no doubt they are guilty of wasting their own time and that of the recipients of countless junk emails they send themselves.

In order to test your own time management skills, complete the following questionnaire.

TIME MANAGEMENT QUESTIONNAIRE

Date____

1. What are the most important results you should achieve

2. What percentage of your time should you spend on these?

3. How much time do you actually spend on these?

4. What are the main causes of wasting your time?

5. How much time do you spend in meetings?

6. Which meetings do you not really need to attend at all or regularly?

7. What tasks could be left undone or done less frequently?

8. How many junk emails do you receive a week internally/externally?

9. What have you done to eliminate junk emails?

Effective time management skills will require that you are happy with 100 per cent. of your answer. Worse still you may not be able to answer some of the questions, which demonstrates that you need to improve your time management. A real tell-tale sign is when you go home having worked hard all day and feeling that you have achieved very little. Most people have no accurate idea of how they spend their working time.

The first step is to record what you do every day, in 15 or 30 minute units as the day progresses, for a period of four weeks. The result is likely to shock you and will spur you into action. It is essential that you record your use of time as it happens, even trying to remember at the end of each day is likely to produce an inaccurate record and it only takes minutes a day to do.

Constantly ask yourself these questions (or a variation on them).

What one thing can I do today that will make a real difference to:

- me
- my family
- my profits
- my soul?

i.e. what can I do today which will have the most impact on the most important elements in my life?

Chairing meetings

Some people are absolutely hopeless at chairing meetings, and the consequences are likely to include a failure to achieve the results or progress required and wasting time as well as causing frustration and demotivation for the people attending. The skills required to chair meetings effectively are easily learned.

To test your ability to chair meetings, complete the following questionnaire.

CHAIRING MEETINGS QUESTIONNAIRE

Date ______________________________

√ or X each box

1. The agenda and any relevant background information are circulated sufficiently well in advance for people to arrive adequately prepared. ☐
2. People know the meeting will start promptly, are expected to arrive on time and are aware of how long the meeting is likely to last. ☐
3. Someone is briefed in advance to introduce each agenda item and to outline the intended scope and result of the discussion. ☐
4. The first item is a review of action completed as minuted at the previous meeting. ☐
5. The most important agenda items are addressed first. ☐
6. You mentally allocate how much time should be spent on each item, and inform people accordingly when appropriate. ☐
7. Only one person speaks at once and undue interruptions are avoided. ☐
8. Waffling, hobby horses and irrelevancies are dealt with firmly but politely. ☐
9. The climate of the meeting is constructive throughout and it finishes on a positive note. ☐
10. The minutes are concise, spell out who will do what by when and are circulated promptly. ☐

If you have scored 10 out of 10, there is every likelihood that you are an outstanding chairman. If your score is much lower, however, do not despair because training usually produces tangible and lasting improvement quickly.

Sales skills

The very thought of being a sales person may be absolute anathema to you, and there is absolutely nothing wrong with that opinion. The reality is, however, that in our working, family and social life we all have to convince and persuade people to agree with us and to take the action we want. This is exactly what sales skills are designed to achieve, so sales skills have the potential to benefit everyone.

Stereotyped images of sales people having 'the gift of the gab' and telling jokes are completely misleading when compared with professional sales skills which anyone can learn and benefit from.

Sales skills involve:

- asking questions to understand what the prospective customer wants to achieve and their concerns
- listening attentively to understand their answers
- acting as a problem solver to find ways to achieve what the customer wants at an affordable price
- flushing out hidden objections and resistance so that these can be overcome
- describing the benefits the prospective customer will gain rather than the features of the product or service
- convincing the prospective customer to buy and to take action by signing a purchase order.

Many customer focussed companies present in-house sales training or enable staff to attend external courses in order to develop a company-wide sales culture. Other companies are prepared to allow staff to attend external courses of their own choosing as long as there is a personal development angle involved. Find out what your company does for staff regarding sales skills training and ask to participate. If there are no opportunities of this kind, videos, CD Roms, websites and books will provide worthwhile basic knowledge and skills.

Personal PR

Whilst many people are concerned to build upon their curriculum vitae, relatively few actively pursue personal PR initiatives. Yet done effectively this can accelerate your career and produce opportunities which would not materialise otherwise.

The initiatives you take need to be approved by your immediate manager or mentor, but should never be described or even referred to as a personal PR initiative because of the likelihood of a negative reaction.

PR is the jargon for public relations and the objective is to achieve favourable awareness of, and publicity for, individuals, companies and other organisations. In a way it is similar to networking with individuals, but involving groups of people or a much wider audience.

Examples of personal PR initiatives you can take include:

- writing a reader's letter to a trade press magazine offering opinion or comment on a topical issue, or writing a response to a previously published letter or feature
- writing a technical article for a trade journal or a relevant website or writing a blog for a relevant website
- entering, and ideally winning a competition such as the Young Engineer of the Year or whatever, nowadays there is almost certainly a competition you could enter
- volunteering to be interviewed for a magazine column which features people with unusual jobs or leisure interests

- joining a working party for your trade association or professional body
- offering to present a session at a relevant conference by approaching conference organisers.
- ensure you use social media such as LinkedIn to network

Once you begin to become known to a wider audience outside your own company, you will be surprised how this generates invitations to do things which will create more personal PR for you. And don't be surprised if it results in headhunters approaching you or receiving job offers from other companies.

Mentoring and coaching

A key ingredient of modern management is mentoring and coaching at every level of an organisation. You may not have thought about it but often the chairman of a company, including global organisations, acts as mentor and coach to the group chief executive.

So you should seek your first opportunity to be a coach and mentor long before you are given a managerial appointment. Many companies have an annual intake of college leavers and university graduates. When you have worked for a year, if your company operates a mentor scheme for new recruits don't wait to be invited to take part, volunteer instead. If there is no mentoring scheme, why not offer your services to your manager to become a mentor to the next person joining your department.

At one level, mentoring and coaching requires common sense and a helpful attitude. Like most skills, however, training and guidance help. Find out about available short training courses, look out for a book on the subject and tap into the Internet to find helpful websites.

Emotional intelligence

The subject of Emotional Intelligence or EI may be unfamiliar to you, but categorically it is not a gimmick. A high emotional intelligence means that you are aware of your own emotions, thoughts and consequent behaviour. When things have gone wrong, or better still are presently going wrong, you have a well developed ability to reflect on and analyse the situation so that it can be corrected quickly and with the least harm done. The heart of emotional intelligence is self-awareness, knowing yourself and having accurate personal insights.

Without adequate self-awareness, you may be unable or unwilling to understand the motives, emotions, anxieties and actions of other people. As a consequence, you could feel that your motives and indeed best intentions towards other people have been misunderstood.

The development of emotional intelligence skills as an important management tool is destined to become widespread, and even commonplace. EI and the ability to understand and control your emotions and recognise and respond to the emotions of others is now rated by some as the single most effective business skill of this new century. More and more information will become available on the subject via the Internet and magazine articles. Training courses exist, so perhaps you should consider jumping on board this bandwagon so that you can add interpersonal effectiveness to self-awareness and sensitivity to work well with other people.

Are you emotionally intelligent?

1	**Emotional awareness** – how aware are you of your emotions – and can you identify how you are feeling – and how they affect your thoughts and actions?	Yes/ No
2	**Self-awareness** – do you know your emotional strengths and weaknesses and do you think about your emotional make-up and reactions, responding well to comments/feedback?	Yes/ No
3	**Self-confidence** – do you have a positive view of your own capabilities so that you can accommodate diverging views and be able to analyse the emotional make-up of others and use your analysis to positive	Yes/ No

Neuro Linguistic Programming (NLP)

Your reaction may be what on earth has NLP got to do with management skills, and there are people who dismiss it as claptrap. Neuro linguistic programming is a body of well researched and developed techniques for understanding, influencing and changing human behaviour. It is a powerful tool which is effective at work, in family relationships and with friends.

There are books, training courses and websites which will help you to learn, use and benefit from NLP techniques. It will almost certainly become much more used in the workplace in the next few years. Your employer is unlikely to dismiss NLP out of hand, so find a suitable course and request that you attend as part of your personal development and offer to report back on techniques you have learned which will benefit the company.

Attention to detail

This may seem an irrelevant skill to highlight, but it is much more important than many people realise. Standards fall with the passage of time, almost as if the law of gravity is at work. Regardless of how brilliant the strategy or concept is, tangible achievement depends upon successful implementation and, above all, attention to every detail. You need to get the message across that it is essential to get every detail right first time, and to keep on repeatedly and relentlessly. When a manager decides to keep quiet about sub-standard work, it is nothing less than overtly condoning mediocrity. Worse still mediocrity has been accepted as the new standard. Getting every detail correct first time is equally important. Correcting mistakes invariably requires more time, work and expense than would have been required to do the task properly in the first place.

No detail is too small to escape scrutiny or to be overlooked. Even a single keystroke in an email sent externally is unacceptable. On one occasion a firm of lawyers was de-appointed from a major project because of keystroke errors in three emails sent early in the assignment. The client took the view that these petty errors smacked of a careless and casual approach, which undermined their confidence. Equally, even a single keystroke error in an internal email is unacceptable, because it could just as easily have been a keystroke error which presented an important figure incorrectly.

This chapter has focussed on developing and improving portable, durable and exploitable skills. Clearly, you have to decide your priorities and the amount of time you are able to devote, but the important thing is to start taking some action now. So fill in your personal skills action plan on the next page.

PERSONAL SKILLS ACTION PLAN

Date ____________________

Action by ____________________

Technology

Speaking skills

Financial knowledge

Industry sector knowledge

Time management skills

Chairing meetings

Sales skills

Personal PR

Mentoring and coaching

Emotional intelligence

Neuro Linguistic Programming

Attention to detail

PART TWO: THE BUSINESS END – ME AT WORK AND ME PLC

CHAPTER

05

MY BRILLIANT CAREER: UP THE ORGANISATION

05

The words of a well known song go something along the lines 'it ain't what you do, but the way that you do it'. This focuses on the fact that it is not only what you achieve and do which singles you out for promotion, but the way you do it can enhance or detract materially. It is important to recognise and develop the traits, behaviour and attitudes which accelerate promotion and career success.

It is also important to:

- write your own job description/career path/job title: in other words do not wait always to be told what is required, but start acting and developing your contribution to the business and you will progress 'up the organisation' – it will adapt to accommodate you rather than you having to fit any existing career progressions
- always reach out and do more than is required
- do not be precious about acting outside your job description (bosses notice 'contribution' at all levels particularly if it is not necessarily in expected areas).

Think, talk and act strategically

Chairmen, chief executives and company directors should think, talk and act strategically all of the time, but the truth is very few do so. Unfortunately, a strategic outlook is not acquired simply or quickly on appointment as a director. It takes years to develop and hopefully the newly appointed director has already spent several years consciously developing these skills.

It can never be too early to understand and learn about strategy as a prelude to beginning to think, talk and act strategically. External training courses, books, business management magazines and the Internet provide plenty of opportunities to learn.

What are some of the characteristics of strategy? Timescale is one; strategy involves taking a medium to long-term outlook and perspective. Equally important is to consider the issues and implications company-wide, and not merely address departmental or functional concerns. Another requirement is to address the external environment which the company will have to adapt to and succeed in rather than be concerned solely with internal management issues.

Some of the aspects of future external environment which need addressing include:

- technology changes which will impact upon the way the industry sector operates, e.g. reducing hardware costs and dramatically greater reliability may mean that maintenance contracts are not renewed and instead the norm becomes never repair equipment but simply replace it with the latest model
- developments in information technology, e.g. the impact of e-commerce on corporate procurement and distribution channels
- environmental issues which could affect the ways and costs of doing business in some industry sectors
- regulatory and legislative changes, e.g. restrictions imposed on the food industry following worldwide outbreaks of BSE in cattle, which may be extended to other animal foods and poultry
- energy and raw material shortages, e.g. oil and electricity even in the developed world
- skill shortages, especially to cope with new technologies
- social change, e.g. the increasing welfare and tax burden caused by the aging population in some countries
- the impact of global mergers on supply and demand
- the upheaval caused by a growing number of local wars and regional conflicts.

Understanding about strategic issues is relatively easy, but developing the inbuilt habit of thinking, talking and acting strategically is another. Thinking strategically requires evaluating change and new ideas not just in terms of the benefit and cost to your department, but thinking through what will be the consequences elsewhere in the company and overall will there be an acceptable benefit and financial return for the company and the shareholders. Talking strategically requires presenting and addressing changes and proposed investments in overall company terms, and demonstrating that you have considered likely changes in the external environment.

To act strategically requires the implementation of decisions which are of strategic importance to the future of the business. The first step is to identify decisions which don't necessarily have to be taken in the immediate future but when made will have a strategic impact. Some examples are as follows:

- a private company where the shareholders are reaching retirement and there are no members of the family to continue. A decision could be made to groom the business for sale in, say, two years time or to strengthen and develop the management team with a view to encouraging a management buy-out in due course
- a listed group with some businesses which are either demonstrably non-core or destined to be low growth, which decides to make a series of divestments
- a medium-sized accountancy firm which lacks strength in various specialist departments and decides to pursue a merger with a complementary firm
- a company providing vending services for beverages only decides to extend into snack vending in order to maximise the potential of the existing customer base.

Volunteer to help your boss

Categorically this is not a suggestion to crawl. The purpose is to widen your experience and take on more responsibility in order to prove your increasing worth and contribution to the business. There may well be some jobs which your boss dislikes doing but are still important. There may be a regular meeting which your boss attends which you could attend instead.

Make yourself 'redundant' and dramatically re-engineer your role

Your reaction may be that to deliberately set out to make yourself redundant is a recipe for unemployment. Not so. People who make themselves redundant are making themselves available for early promotion, and are often promoted accordingly. Contrast it with the situation where you have made yourself either indispensable or very difficult to replace. In these circumstances, your boss is more likely to block your promotion or transfer.

Techniques which you can use to make yourself redundant, or at least partially so in order that you can dramatically re-engineer your role include:

- using information technology developments to materially increase your productivity or to enable you to de-skill your job so that a less qualified or experienced person can do the work
- simplify your role or join with colleagues to re-engineer the wider business process
- train and develop members of your team to take over as much of your role as possible

Get the important soft issues right

Some people produce results which amply merit promotion but get overlooked or see people with less tangible achievement moving up the organisation ahead of them. Often the reason is several instances of getting the soft issues wrong, because these can and do have a substantial bearing on promotion.

Reliability is a virtue, the lack of it is at the very least annoying and irritating, and it comes in the following guises:

- always being prompt for both internal and external meetings, as opposed to attracting comments such as 'kind of you to join us at last'
- when given a deadline to complete a task, raising any concerns you have at the outset such as conflicting priorities or lack of resources and dealing with them, otherwise reliably meeting the deadline. Occasionally, subsequent events may mean that either you cannot meet the deadline or there is a risk of slipping. In these circumstances, it is vital that you notify people promptly and suggest the additional help or resources you need in order to meet the deadline after all. Set out to gain the reputation that everything you agree to do, however small it may be, will be done well and on time
- make sure that you engage your brain before putting your mouth into gear, not only at meetings but in informal one-to-one discussions. Become regarded as the person who is always worth listening to because your ideas have been thought through rather than viewed as someone who comes up with half-baked ideas or fails to stick to the subject
- demonstrate loyalty not only to your manager, but equally to your colleagues at every level in the team

- be ready to volunteer when people ask for help and, better still, offer help when you sense someone is struggling
- criticise people to their face, not behind their back. Seek to understand their situation and feelings with a view to calmly and constructively resolving differences
- develop and exhibit poise, particularly when under pressure or you are provoked. Getting rattled or making an outburst undermines the confidence people have in you because they will have an understandable concern that you behave unpredictably and inappropriately
- always act impeccably with external people, whether it is being on the receiving end of a customer complaint, even if not justified in your opinion, or having entirely valid grounds to criticise a supplier.

Volunteer for working parties and project teams

Companies often use temporary working parties, project teams or task forces to re-engineer business processes, to specify and implement new technology, to deal with a short-term major problem or to handle a one-off situation such as office relocation. Some working parties are doomed to be ineffective either because the leader is ineffective or perhaps internal politics will sabotage progress, so be selective about which working parties you volunteer to join but the potential benefits to you include:

- gaining wider experience
- working with people who may be more senior than your immediate manager, and becoming noticed
- being associated with an important project
- possibly being promoted to fill a new role which has emerged from the project.

Show leadership

You may feel that you have no opportunity to demonstrate your leadership qualities because you do not manage a staff of your own. However, there are invariably opportunities to lead. Consider the following examples:

- you are one of a small group of, say, engineers or research analysts who share a team assistant. To avoid conflicting priorities and to ensure that the assistant really is part of the team, you could suggest a weekly meeting of everyone to ensure priorities are agreed and the assistant understands what the team has to achieve
- you have a full-time assistant but spend a lot of your time out of the office attending client meetings. You should develop the habit of a regular weekly meeting not only to discuss the work to be done in the coming week, but to address how to communicate and work together more effectively.

Leadership is hard to define in a meaningful way, but is something which people instinctively recognise as being effective or poor. The ingredients of effective leadership include:

- induction of new staff, making sure that people are welcomed, introduced to colleagues, and given the basic training and background required for their job
- involving the whole team in setting the future direction and goals
- encouraging people to come forward with ideas and improvements, and to challenge the status quo
- creating a climate whereby people raise their problems and concerns and fully expect them to be addressed

- ensuring that workloads and rewards are equitable within the team
- regularly saying thank you for a job well done and giving praise whenever deserved
- adopting a coaching and mentoring style of management rather than the outdated approach of instruct and control
- providing opportunities for learning new skills, personal development and a broadening work experience.

Develop your decision-making skills

Sound decision-making skills are vital for career success. Furthermore, it is not enough to be good at making the decisions which have to be made because you are faced with an immediate need to do so. Often the decisions which have the greatest impact are those which do not have to be made in the foreseeable future. These are the decisions which help you to steal a march on your competitors or be the first to seize an opportunity and to achieve a dominant strength as a result.

Consider impending food regulations that will seriously affect the production processes and costs of the whole industry sector and force some smaller competitors out of business. Rather than waiting for the anticipated legislation to become law, a strategic decision may be made that the company will implement the necessary changes voluntarily and use this as a platform for advertising and public relations campaigns to increase market share.

At an operational level, a company may find that skilled staff are becoming harder to recruit and retain because of a serious shortage affecting the industry sector. A contributory factor facing a company could be that their office location and premises are below par. One approach would be to struggle on, but a decision which could be made is to invest in new offices which make a positive contribution to staff recruitment and retention.

Effective decision-making involves the following steps:

- identifying what the core problem is rather than simply addressing the visible symptoms
- recognising the consequences and problems which may occur elsewhere and ensuring these become part of the solution
- developing outline alternative solutions, and using team members to brainstorm ideas if appropriate, before falling in love with a particular solution
- developing the chosen alternative to identify and address the consequences and implications
- formulating the specification required for any equipment and software to be procured
- obtaining alternative quotations, together with evaluating the financial stability and customer service of possible suppliers
- making a financial evaluation of the proposed expenditure and savings by projecting the incremental cash flows from the project to enable a discounted cash flow analysis to be done
- preparing an implementation programme
- monitoring the benefits actually achieved to test the success of the project and to make necessary improvements.

Be a resultaholic not a workaholic

Workaholics are not necessarily effective people. As the name implies, they are addicted to work. The reality is that few people can work effectively for more than 55 hours a week on a sustained basis.

Test yourself by answering the following questions.

Do you:

- regularly work more than 55 hours a week?
- take work home in the evenings and at weekends?
- go into the office most weekends?
- often make work related calls from home in the evening and at weekends?
- talk about work whenever you are with friends?

If you have answered yes to one of the above questions, it is quite possible that you are a workaholic, and two or more yes answers is confirmation that you are one despite any protestations you make. Remember, no alcoholic will accept that they are an alcoholic until they join Alcoholics Anonymous or enter a clinic.

If you choose to be a resultaholic you will achieve significantly more and spend materially less time working. In addition, you will suffer less stress, your family relationships will improve and you will have more leisure time.

To become a resultaholic requires the following action:

- decide which results and tasks are most important, and allocate sufficient time for them

- decide which tasks do not need doing at all, can be done less frequently, or can be delegated to another team member
- decide which meetings you do not really need to attend, or you attend purely by habit or to 'keep informed'. Either send someone else to attend or simply read the minutes
- have your name deleted from the circulation list of minutes and monthly reports, which you do not need, and ruthlessly stop unwanted emails at source
- politely decline lunch and evening invitations unless the benefit amply justifies the time involved or you will enjoy the people and the occasion

In this way, you will eliminate at least 10 hours work a week, and many workaholics can save 20 or even 30 hours a week.

You should also consider whether you are guilty of 'presenteeism' and, if you think you could be more productive working from home, don't be afraid to ask to do so.

In order to translate good intentions into tangible improvement, complete the following action plan.

SUCCESS TRAITS ACTION PLAN

Date ____

Action by ____

Think, talk and act strategically

Volunteer to help your boss

Make yourself redundant or re-engineer your role

Get the soft issues right

Volunteer for working parties and project teams

Show leadership

Develop decision-making skills

Be a resultaholic, not a workaholic

CHAPTER

06

STARTING YOUR OWN BUSINESS

06

The decision to start any business should not be taken lightly or quickly, and is not the right decision for everyone. The failure rate of new businesses is staggeringly high. Many are started with inadequate finance, compounded by overoptimistic assumptions of early success, and simply fail because the cash runs out. New restaurants have a high failure rate within the first twelve months of opening.

Typically, a chef dreams of opening a restaurant but has no financial knowledge. Premises are located, the kitchen is just about adequate but the chef indulges in an expensive dream kitchen. Belatedly, because of the time required to complete the refit of the kitchen, the restaurant opens and in the meantime the chef has had to use some savings for living expenses. Then diners are slow to come, and some will not return. It may be necessary to offer discounted set price meals to attract people, but margins will have been slashed. Just when the restaurant is becoming popular, the cash runs out, the bank will not increase the overdraft and the restaurant fails.

Another reason why starting a business is unsuitable for some people is that it requires a variety of skills and roles which may be unpalatable. In the early days, the owner has to:

- find suitable premises and negotiate a lease/service agreement
- go out and sell the products or services
- organise a bank loan or find other sources of finance
- negotiate with suppliers
- cope with accountancy, taxes and business software
- handle regulatory requirements such as employment law
- recruit, train and manage staff
- and, not least, do whatever else needs doing.

Despite the hazards and risks involved, perhaps you are still determined to become self-employed or start your own business. Fine. The important thing is to start with your eyes wide open and to set out in a way which will minimise the risk and consequences of failure. Creating a successful business is likely to create dramatically more wealth for you and your family than a highly paid career ever will.

Low-risk start-up

One low risk way to start self-employment or to create a business is to launch it in your spare time whilst continuing with your paid employment. Consider someone doing a monotonous job, but with a passion and a talent for woodcarving. One product could be to carve birds. A low risk approach would be to carve a small stock and then visit, say, local pub restaurants to persuade them to display the products on a sale or return basis. It offers the pub restaurant a chance to make some extra income, by taking a commission on sales, for no outlay and risk free. Within twelve months, it should have become clear that either the income potential is sufficient to become worthwhile self-employment or that it will be at best a modest source of spare time income.

To start on a part-time basis may simply not be feasible. So if a full-time commitment is required, a way to ensure that the range of skills required is available is to start a business with other people who have complementary skills. A 'general understanding' between the people involved may cause major disagreement, litigation or even the break-up of the venture at a later stage. Either a basic partnership agreement prepared by a solicitor is required or an accountant can form an 'off-the-shelf' limited liability company for you. The cost should be less than one thousand pounds and is essential expenditure. It would be folly to decide to delay until the business can afford the expense involved, by then serious and irreparable damage may have been done.

The choice of which business to start will have a major influence on success or failure. Possible sources of business opportunities include:

- a leisure activity skill or expertise could eventually become full-time self-employment, e.g. photography, curtain making, painting and decorating. It must be realised, however, that a passion for photography and a knowledge of camera equipment does not equip someone to open a photographic shop without any previous experience of the retail trade. Some people have succeeded, despite making expensive mistakes initially, but more have failed
- offer to outsource for your present employer. Perhaps half of your time is spent writing a company newsletter, which you thoroughly enjoy, and the rest of the time involves miscellaneous administrative work. You could explain that you want to pursue a full-time writing career, but rather than leave the company you would prefer to write the newsletter for a fixed monthly fee on a self-employed basis and use the remaining time to find other writing work. Outsourcing is so commonplace today that many companies will respond positively. You will need to find freelance writing opportunities for magazines, perhaps by submitting work on a speculative basis, or approach other companies offering to write their newsletters on a contract basis
- becoming a franchisee. Franchising is a huge industry in most developed countries and there are hundreds of opportunities to choose from, ranging from major brands such as McDonalds to operations designed to make a quick fortune for the franchisor at the expense of franchisees.

Becoming a franchisee

Choosing a proven and suitable franchise is of the essence. Banks are a useful source of information because some specialise in financing franchisees and consequently have a wealth of first hand information about the actual profitability or otherwise of various franchise opportunities. Franchise associations, the Internet and relevant websites, special features in newspapers and franchise exhibitions are other sources of useful information. Once you have identified several franchise operations which appeal to you and which suit your skills and experience, the following questions need to be answered:

- when was the franchise operation started?
- who owns the company and has there been a recent change of ownership?
- is the company financially stable? You need someone to obtain the most recent annual report to establish that the company is not deteriorating or facing the risk of receivership
- how many franchised operations have been created each year?
- have any franchisees failed?
- how many franchisees have sold their franchise, and did they realise a capital profit or loss? How many are presently trying to sell their franchise?
- what are the audited profits of both recently opened and well established franchises?
- what training and marketing support is provided?

A reputable franchisor will provide a dossier of reliable information. Verification is essential, and one of the best ways to do this is to talk to a cross section of franchise owners.

Buying an existing business

An alternative to starting a business is to buy one. There is ample choice. National, local and trade press carry advertisements, websites offer businesses for sale, business transfer agents and business brokers maintain registers of businesses for sale. The first step is to decide the type and location of a business to buy, in keeping with your financial resources, skills and experience. Then get details of the various businesses for sale which appear to meet your requirements. Before falling in love with a particular business remember the expression 'let the buyer beware'. Rigorous scrutiny is essential. Some of the issues to be addressed include:

- although a firm of accountants may have prepared the accounts of a sole trader or audited the accounts of a small limited liability company, the accuracy of the figures is heavily dependant upon the records and information prepared by the owners. You really need an accountant to verify that the figures are accurate, in other words to establish that the turnover has not been overstated or the costs incurred by the business understated to justify the selling price for the business
- if monthly management accounts are not prepared, it is difficult to get a reliable picture of financial performance after the end of the previous financial year, and the business may have deteriorated in the meantime
- the sales to major customers may be dependent upon a longstanding and close personal friendship with the vendors
- annual or longer term customer contracts may be due for renewal shortly, and may be lost to a competitor
- a major competitive threat is known to the vendors to be a distinct possibility. For example, a major supermarket chain is seeking to purchase a site close to an independent delicatessen

- a key supplier is facing financial difficulties and it will not be easy to find an alternative source of supply

There is no ready-made checklist to ensure that every eventuality and contingency has been covered. The approach required is to identify the key factors for success and the main vulnerabilities which could exist, and then rigorously evaluate them.

A solicitor will be needed to prepare a purchase and sale agreement on behalf of the purchasers, including suitable warranties and indemnities to provide protection. It would be foolish, however, to think that contractual terms are a substitute for thorough investigation because litigation is time-consuming, expensive and does not offer guaranteed reimbursement.

Going the Management Buy-Out (MBO) route

A much more attractive and financially rewarding opportunity is to purchase the business which employs you, provided the owners agree, by completing a management buy-out. These are often backed by a venture capital or private equity house, but in certain circumstances it may be possible to finance the purchase using only debt finance and this would enable the management team to own 100 per cent. of the share capital.

In the UK, the remainder of Europe and the USA there is a veritable mountain of money available for management buy-outs (MBOs). Hundreds of MBOs take place each year in the UK alone, and arguably the shortage is in quality management teams rather than available financing.

Before enquiring about or requesting the opportunity to pursue an MBO there needs to be a committed management team in place. Private equity houses strongly prefer to back a management team led by an experienced managing director, and in the case of a group subsidiary company this should not present a problem. Private companies probably have the title of managing director occupied by one of the owners, but it is possible that the leader of the team already has profit responsibility as a divisional or subsidiary company managing director. If not, then the case will have to be presented that the MBO leader had substantial de facto profit responsibility without the title of managing director.

The next step is to establish there is a top management team committed to pursuing an MBO, typically no more than three or four people, and including a finance person. If one key person does not wish to invest in the MBO, then it is still possible to proceed but with a stated commitment to fill the vacancy with someone prepared to invest, with recruitment commencing during the MBO process so that an appointment can be made on legal completion or soon afterwards. If there is no suitable managing director to lead the team it is much more of a problem because it is difficult for the team to find their own leader.

The typical investment required from each member of the buy-out team is about six month's salary, and probably a minimum of £50,000. The managing director is often invited to invest a third to a half more than other team members in order to benefit from a bigger equity stake. People may need to take a second mortgage on their home to finance their investment, but the potential capital gain makes it worthwhile. Most management buy-outs result in an exit by a trade sale or stockmarket listing within three to five years, and typical capital gains for the management team range from 20 to 80 times their original investment. No-one should ever imagine, however, that a buy-out is a guaranteed financial bonanza, some buy-outs do end up in receivership which means that management will lose the cash they invested and probably their jobs as well.

A request to pursue a management buy-out needs handling carefully, especially if the business is underperforming. The group or private owners may mistakenly think that the management team have allowed the business to underperform in order to reduce the purchase price. In some cases a request to pursue an MBO has lead to a swift dismissal of the team leader, so care really is needed. One way to minimise the risk is to meet a corporate finance boutique or an accountancy firm and, without appointing them or incurring any costs, get them to:

- assess the feasibility of finding financial backing for an MBO
- telephone the group or private owners, 'on behalf of a client', to find out if there is any prospect of considering an offer to buy the business. If not, the management team need to shelve the idea for the foreseeable future, but otherwise they can make a tactful approach with some confidence

If a management team were to approach a private equity house and to disclose financial information about the business, without the express permission of the owners, there are grounds for and a real risk of summary dismissal. Consequently, private equity houses are reluctant to involve themselves with management teams in these circumstances because they are at risk of litigation for soliciting a purchase without permission.

Every management team needs a corporate finance adviser to pursue a management buy-out because of the complexity and amount of work involved. Probably three prospective advisers should be interviewed and asked the following questions:

- how many buy-outs has the firm, and most importantly the person you meet, completed of a similar size and complexity?

- will the senior person you meet lead the transaction demonstrably from the front throughout?
- how many of their buy-outs have failed and why?
- which private equity houses have invested in buy-outs they have advised upon? (to make sure they do not favour particular houses to win reciprocal business for themselves)
- what will you do to ensure we obtain the maximum equity stake for our investment?
- will you negotiate the purchase of the business for us from the owners?
- may we have the names and telephone numbers of three people for whom you have advised on their buy-out? (There is no substitute for telephone references on the individual advisers.)
- are you prepared to invest some or all of your fee in the buy-out on the same terms as the private equity house? (A real test of their commitment.)

The corporate finance adviser should select four relevant private equity houses and contact them. Obtain a written offer from each, and negotiate approved offers before the investor is selected. The new company set up to buy the business, referred to as 'newco', will pay all the professional costs on legal completion, but it is vital that the management team do not incur any unexpected costs if the buy-out is not completed for any reason.

Develop a winning business plan

The business plan needs to convince the investor that the proposed buy-out is an attractive investment. It is primarily a selling document and should demonstrate the management team's commitment to the buy-out and the subsequent development of the business.

The business plan should be written by the management team. Their financial advisor should provide a critical and constructive review of the plan and the financial projections. The plan should ideally be no more than 15 to 25 pages long, plus appendices.

A typical business plan should include:

- an executive summary, preferably no longer than one page, covering the main points and setting out the situation with the vendors and the amount of finance required
- a concise history of the business and a description of the products or services, markets served, distribution channels, location and size
- an analysis of the market and the competitive position of the business
- a description of the main assets and any key features of the way the business operates
- a profile of the management team, their positions and responsibilities, their qualifications and experience plus an overview of the staff
- summary results over the last two or three years and projections for the next three years showing profit and loss, cash flow and balance sheets

The projections should be positive, credible and specific. Where the projections show rapid growth or a change in the nature of operations, the background and reasoning will need to be clearly spelled out.

An indication of likely acquisition cost should be included if known, together with any further funding requirements. It is generally not appropriate to outline funding structure.

Typically, the stages involved and the likely sequence of events are:

- agree on members of the management buy-out team, and the choice of managing director
- select and appoint financial advisers to the management team
- assess whether the opportunity is suitable for a buy-out
- obtain approval or accept the invitation to pursue a management buy-out, if the opportunity is suitable
- determine or evaluate the vendor's asking price
- write the business plan
- meet three or four carefully selected equity investors
- obtain written offers of financial backing from each investor
- appoint legal advisers to the management
- select the preferred lead investor
- negotiate the best possible equity deal for the management
- negotiate the purchase of the business, with a cost indemnity and a period of exclusivity
- carry out due diligence using investigating accountants
- obtain debt finance and syndicate equity investment if necessary
- prepare and negotiate legal documents
- achieve legal completion

Most buy-outs take up to six months. When buying from a receiver, speed is essential and the equity investor will respond accordingly. Private equity houses occasionally publish case histories showing a management buy-out legally completing within three months. These are the exceptions.

A typical timetable of events is:

Month 1

- agree on the management team;
- appoint financial advisers;
- obtain agreement to pursue a management buy-out.

Month 2

- write the business plan and send it to equity investors;
- hold initial meetings with prospective equity investors;
- seek a cost indemnity and period of exclusivity.

Month 3

- obtain outline written offers from prospective equity investors;
- negotiate improved terms with equity investors;
- appoint preferred equity investor and lawyers;

Month 4

- negotiate the acquisition from the vendors;
- sign heads of agreement;
- investigating accountants complete due diligence.

Month 5/6

- equity investor syndicates equity if appropriate;
- arrange debt finance;
- prepare and negotiate legal documents;
- renegotiate the equity deal for management, if necessary;
- legally complete the management buy-out as soon as possible.

Throughout this period, the management team must continue to manage the business, or suffer the consequences immediately after the management buy-out is completed. The financial advisers must take the brunt of the workload connected with the management buy-out.

Expert advice is needed before the management buy-out is legally completed in order to ensure the maximum benefit for the management team after paying income and capital gains tax.

Issues that need to be addressed are:

- the availability of income tax relief on the interest paid on borrowings to purchase an equity stake
- legitimate opportunities to minimise capital gains tax and inheritance tax liabilities in due course under current taxation regulations
- income tax relief on the purchase price of the equity stake should the business fail after the management buy-out

When a subsidiary is being acquired from a group, the employees will cease to be members of the group pension scheme at, or shortly after, legal completion. The management buy-out team will need to take actuarial advice prior to legal completion to ensure that the value of the pension fund to be transferred to

Newco will be sufficient to meet the pension liabilities for the staff to be employed.

If the group pension scheme is underfunded, this could involve Newco making significant additional contributions to meet the liability. Equally, this could mean either that a lower acquisition price would need to be negotiated or the management buy-out would not be completed. Conversely, if the group pension scheme is overfunded, the transfer of a share of the surplus should be sought in order to benefit from a 'pension contribution holiday' for a period.

When share capital is acquired, the contracts of employment for staff will normally continue unchanged. As mentioned previously, however, the equity investor will want to establish new contracts for the key managers investing in the buy-out.

Where the assets and business are acquired, the Transfer of Undertakings (Protection of Employment) Regulations are likely to apply. These are complex regulations, and one provision is that, unless the terms of employment are substantially unchanged, then Newco could face claims for redundancy payments from staff.

Acquirers of all kinds – corporates or venture capital-backed management teams – are becoming aware of the environmental pitfalls that can affect transactions. However, equity and debt providers funding a buy-out will be particularly sensitive to any environmental issues that might arise. Their concern will extend beyond the business having all the necessary approvals, permits and licences necessary to operate and will include the state of the fabric of any buildings and of any surrounding property. Funders will wish to establish any manner in which any property assets over which security may be granted may be affected by environmental issues as well as any liabilities which might be incurred by Newco or indeed, the funders themselves.

UK environmental legislation can make both occupiers, owners and 'polluters' liable for environmental problems. As a minimum, most funders will insist on a 'Phase One' environmental investigation of a business with manufacturing or property assets, which adds to the timetable.

Newco pays all fees on legal completion as the cost of the acquisition.

The equity investor and the debt providers are likely to charge an arrangement fee of between one and two per cent of the total funding requirement.

As the equity investor will appoint lawyers to act for Newco and the investigating accountants to carry out due diligence, the management's financial advisers should establish that the equity investor is responsible for these fees if the management buy-out is not legally completed, unless covered by a cost indemnity for the vendors.

The financial advisers and lawyers to the management team will often be working almost wholly on a contingent basis, their fees dependent on legal completion except for cost indemnities negotiated from the vendors.

The management team must ensure they are not personally liable for unexpected and sizeable fees, plus VAT, if the management buy-out does not legally complete. This is an important issue for the financial advisers to address.

Even though the fees for the various advisers to the management team will be paid by Newco on legal completion, the cost of fees should be agreed in writing at the earliest possible opportunity.

Managing the business effectively must become the top priority immediately after legal completion.

The equity investor will probably want to appoint a chairman or non-executive director. Some private equity investors tend to put the person who led the deal for them onto the board. Others will opt for an outsider, usually with relevant industry experience. If the chemistry is not right with the first candidate put forward, then the management team should ask to meet a second one.

The management team should consider carefully the extent to which they will seek additional capital following the buy-out either to fund organic growth or acquisition. In a significant number of cases, it is the avowed intention of the management team to embark upon a 'buy and build strategy' and this needs to be reflected in the whole buy-out process.

In the first instance the requirement for follow-on funding should be addressed within the business plan. Where the requirement for follow-on funding can be identified with certainty, the amount required and the anticipated returns should be included within the financial projections. Where a number of opportunities are being considered or where there is uncertainty as to timing or amount, the general principle should be within the business plan with the financial projection per se concentrating on the stand-alone business.

As a rule, private equity houses and banks welcome the opportunity to provide follow-on funding. In all cases, the appetite for follow-on funding should be established at an early stage together with some degree of common understanding with regards to purpose, amount and likely risk/benefit.

Consider a Management Buy-In (MBI) route

If there is no opportunity to pursue an MBO, because the owners will not agree, then the management team could pursue a management buy-in (MBI) of another business. This is somewhat more difficult to achieve because the team will probably need to keep their present jobs in the meantime. Also, approaches the team makes directly to purchase a business will be viewed sceptically because they will have to find financial backing. Ideally, the team should research suitable target businesses in their own time and ask a corporate finance adviser to make an approach in order to have sufficient credibility, without incurring any cost.

A successful chief executive of a substantial company could pursue a different approach by resigning, or perhaps being made redundant because of a takeover, and pursuing a management buy-in opportunity on a full-time basis. Finding a suitable business available to buy at an acceptable price is the key to success, and it makes sense to work exclusively with one firm of corporate finance advisers prepared to dedicate resources on a speculative basis to find an opportunity and legally complete a deal. Without a dedicated search, the risk faced by the buy-in executive is that available cash is used up and it becomes necessary to take another job.

Whether you are buying an established business, possibly via an MBO or MBI, or starting a new business, then a convincing business plan is a prerequisite to obtaining financial backing. The statistics are daunting. Private equity houses reject 70 per cent. of business plans without even meeting the management team, and typically invest in only 1 per cent. of the businesses for which plans are submitted.

Research the market rigorously

If you are starting a new business, a rigorous assessment of your potential market and existing competition is overwhelmingly important. A 'suck it and see' approach is tantamount to gambling. If the business depends upon people visiting the premises, then location, location and location are three of the most important factors for success. Factors affecting your choice of location should include:

- does the proposed location attract sufficient passing pedestrians?
- does the street or development have other premises which attract the kind of people who are likely to be your potential customers?
- is there ample car parking nearby or is adjacent parking a problem?
- if the previous business on the site closed down, why and was it a similar business?
- is the street or location increasing in popularity or is it in decline and are there vacant shops?
- what development or redevelopment plans and applications, or road improvement schemes could affect the location?
- where are similar businesses, discount stores and supermarkets located which will affect your business?
- if the site is on the edge of a town or located out of town, what will persuade people to make the effort to visit your premises?
- what is the online performance/potential?

Setting aside location, the size of the market must be addressed. Consider someone planning to open an upmarket bespoke curtain making business in a small market town. Questions to be answered include:

- what is the minimum value of annual sales when the business is established for financial viability?
- how many typical customers will be required to produce this level of sales?
- how many homes in the town are potential buyers of upmarket curtains?
- what percentage of these homes would need to buy curtains from you each year to achieve the required sales turnover?
- does this percentage seem realistic?
- assuming there is no other curtain shop in the town, what other well-established and similar shops are located in nearby towns?
- if so, why should people travel from one of these towns to buy from your shop?
- is there a major store in a nearby large town offering a bespoke curtain making service at much lower prices?
- what other related products could you stock to increase the overall sales and to persuade more customers to visit your shop, e.g. lamps, cushions, glass vases etc.

Find the finance

To start your own business it is likely that you will need to raise finance, assuming that help from relatives has been ruled out. Your existing bank is a good place to start. Belief, passion and self confidence are important, but rarely ever sufficient to convince a bank manager to provide start-up finance. Your business plan is the key to success. The bank manager will judge your request for finance by considering:

- what you have done to research and quantify the market
- how your product or service is better, different or cheaper than other suppliers offer
- how you will advertise, promote and sell your business from a standing start
- whether your sales projections, especially during the first year, are realistic
- how much cash you are investing and the salary or drawings you intend to take
- what safety margin is built into your cash flow projections to survive if sales are disappointing
- what relevant skills you have which will help you to succeed, or are there necessary skills and experience you lack

One of the most effective ways to accumulate capital is to start a business or to pursue a buy-out or buy-in. One of the easiest things to do, however, is to find excuses for delaying for the time being. Yet successful entrepreneurs so often say 'I wish that I had started a business many years earlier'. The era of the serial entrepreneur has already arrived. In the same way that people are likely to have different careers and to work for several different companies, the successful entrepreneur is likely to start or own several businesses by selling one and repeating the process.

If you really want to be self-employed or to own your own business, the time to take action is now and the starting point should be to complete the following action plan.

BUSINESS START UP ACTION PLAN

Date ____________________

Action to be taken within one month

____

____

____

Action to be taken within three months

____

____

____

Action to be taken within six months

____

____

____

Results to be achieved within 12 months

____

____

____

PART THREE: KNOWING ME, KNOWING YOU

three

CHAPTER

07

HELL IS OTHER PEOPLE

07

‘Hell is other people’ (JP Sartre), but it certainly needn’t be that way. Working effectively and career success both depend heavily upon getting the support and co-operation of other people. One way to look at the situation is to consciously build a wide fan club of people whom you can rely upon and who will be ready to offer help, rather than seek to avoid you or are always ‘busy’ when you would like help.

Get feedback

It is entirely possible, indeed remarkably commonplace, to spend a lot of time talking with someone on a continuing basis and never to really communicate with each other. Their reaction to you, their personal feelings, anxieties, aspirations and motivation may remain a closed book to you. If so, it is akin to putting on a blindfold to materially hamper yourself and it simply need not be so. The solution is to welcome and actively seek feedback.

Your present job, how well you perform and more importantly what your boss or mentor thinks of you is likely to have a considerable bearing on what job you get next and when. Although many companies rightly provide training to help managers conduct assessment interviews or to write assessment reports, many people still feel uncomfortable and reticent. Consequently, they may pull their punches with you but be candid about you to their manager and other senior colleagues. You must prevent this happening by requesting candid feedback, especially if the company does not have a regular appraisal procedure. You should tell your boss that because you really want to do an outstanding job and to be a highly valued team player, you want candid feedback along the following lines:

- in what ways do you need to improve the results you achieve and the work you do?
- specifically, what do you need to do to improve the results you achieve and the way you work?
- what else should you be doing or not doing?
- how can you work more effectively to support your boss?
- what training, new skills or personal development should you be pursuing?
- are you seen as a team player who works effectively with the rest of the team? If not, how do you need to change your approach?
- should you be taking on any additional responsibilities, acting as a mentor to a recent joiner or joining a working party?

Of course, there may well be ideas or suggestions which you would like to explore during the discussion and these should be raised so that it is a two-way conversation. You should consider at the end of the conversation volunteering to reflect on what has been discussed and to commit to email what you intend to achieve and to do as a result of the meeting.

Feedback from your colleagues is valuable as well, but needs to be handled in a different way. For example, by inviting feedback on certain issues in informal surroundings such as at lunch or over a drink after work. The questions need posing more informally as well, but aspects to be raised could include:

- ways in which you can or need to become a better team player
- things you do which annoy or irritate other people

- what you can learn from other colleagues
- how you are viewed by other people, not just colleagues but more junior support staff as well.

An effective relationship with support staff is important and valuable, because senior staff need and benefit from their help which cannot be taken for granted. It is a fact of life that support staff will most readily help those people whom they like and who treat them with respect and courtesy. When your assistant is on holiday or ill, you may have to rely on someone else to stand in and this provides plenty of scope to be too busy to provide the help you need. A little appreciation always goes a long way, so make a point of always saying 'thank you'.

If you feel that a member of the support staff acts in an unhelpful way towards you or is offhand, take it upon yourself to be responsible for coolly and calmly finding out what is causing the apparent problem and how the two of you, but especially you, can work constructively and enjoyably together.

Manage your boss

To manage your boss is easier said than done, and it certainly does not mean dumping your work on the boss. It does mean finding what makes the person tick, in other words:

- what personal ambitions does your boss have?
- what results, reputation and role is your boss striving to achieve?
- what anxieties, problems, pressures and stress does he/she face?
- does he/she feel secure or under threat?

- what are his/her family circumstances and do these have a significant bearing on work?
- how does he/she prefer to manage people?
- what tasks and responsibilities would he/she like to drop, and does this provide an opportunity for you?
- how could you be most helpful?

Clearly, it would not be politic to formally 'interview' your boss in the office to obtain this information. It needs to be done informally, probably piecemeal, and perhaps out of the office when travelling together or having a drink after work.

So what is the point of this, you may ask. It should enable you to build a stronger rapport, to provide opportunities to enhance your role and contribution and to develop a mutually compatible way of working together. Similarly, if you manage staff then the techniques described so far in this chapter will help you to manage your team more effectively.

Manage your business bank manager effectively

The attitude that the business bank manager is the supplier and you are the customer is fine, provided that you will never need support and help in order to keep your business afloat. Arguably, however, it is shortsighted and myopic. The most effective way to get help and support from your business bank manager when you really are in need is to maintain a personal contact and to provide relevant information including:

- even if your present overdraft facility is sufficient for the year ahead, send your bank manager a copy of your profit and loss and cash flow budgets, calendarised in monthly intervals. When you do need a larger overdraft facility, your business bank manager should be more receptive because you have established a pattern of reliable cash flow budgeting

- consider sending a copy of your quarterly management accounts to demonstrate that the business is performing satisfactorily. This is particularly important when your overdraft is close to the limit of your facility
- always notify your business bank manager BEFORE exceeding your agreed overdraft limit, either by telephone or meeting, and explain the reasons and indicate how quickly you expect to be back within your limit
- make a point of sending a copy of your annual audited accounts
- meet your business bank manager at least annually to discuss your overdraft requirements for the next year, to provide an update on the performance and development of the business, to find out any new products or improved overdraft rates and bank charges which can benefit you
- do not change banks lightly, because the length of your banking relationship may, but not necessarily, help when you really need their support. If you are dissatisfied with your banking arrangements, approach other banks and obtain written proposals. Then approach your own bank and invite them to match or better the terms on the grounds that you have no wish to change banks.

Manage your private equity house

The management team may well own the majority of the ordinary and voting share capital, and the private equity investor the remaining minority. This is not a case of majority rule, however, because there will be a shareholders' agreement which gives substantial rights and protection to the private equity house.

The most important step is to choose the private equity house carefully. When meeting private equity houses initially they will be assessing the management team, but it is equally important to ask them the following questions:

- what involvement will you have in the company provided that performance is in line with budget?
- will you want to appoint a chairman and/or a non-executive director?
- will the person handling the investment for the private equity house be appointed as a non-executive director?

If the answer to the second two questions is a definitive yes and for some reason the management team have taken a personal dislike then a different solution has got to be found at the outset, or a different investor selected.

- if the chairman and/or non-executive director are to be external appointments, may the management team propose suitable candidates or recommend the candidate profile which would add most benefit?
- which major decisions will require specific approval of the private equity house?

- if the business performs less than satisfactorily what intervention will the private equity house take?
- may you speak to three companies which they have invested in to find out their experience?

Some management teams react emotionally to the prospect of a non-executive director being appointed and expressions such as 'a costly spy in the camp' have been used. Whilst the chairman or non-executive director will have a duty to keep the investor informed of progress and to supply budget and monthly management accounts information, there is an opportunity to select someone who will make a valuable contribution to the success of the business.

If an executive from the private equity house is to become a non-executive director, there is the potential to introduce other investee companies as prospective customers and possibly to benefit from a personal network of senior and influential business people. When an external non-executive appointment is to be made there is an opportunity to agree a candidate profile which will bring most benefit to the business and then to search for suitable and compatible candidates.

Manage your professional advisers

Professional advisers may include auditors, solicitors, tax advisers, public relations experts, pensions specialists and so on. Predictably, a crucial step is to choose appropriate advisers in the first place and questions to be asked include:

- how typical a client are you in terms of the help wanted, your size and the likely annual fee? Your business needs to be sufficiently attractive to receive the continuing involvement of the senior person you meet and equally you should not be their largest or most demanding client because otherwise they may be learning at your expense

- how much information have they collected about your company prior to meeting you? E.g. visited your website, obtained your annual accounts, done a press cutting search
- have they any clients in the industry sector which could be of benefit or a potential conflict?
- what pro-active ideas do they mention? or are they purely reactive advisers?
- what case histories can they present which demonstrate the expertise you want?
- is their real skill conceptual ideas and strategy formulation? Or predominantly implementation or both? And which do you need?
- which relevant clients can you telephone to obtain personal references on the senior person who will be your lead adviser? Relevance is important; if you are a private company appointing public relations advisers then outstanding references from a government agency and a listed company are not only irrelevant, but may indicate lack of private company clients.

Manage your major customers and clients

Whenever top management loses contact with major customers or clients, there is a real danger that they are out of touch with the business. Major customers are demanding and have a right to be, they can often provide an early indication of changing needs and ways of doing business which is unlikely to be learned by the operational people servicing the account until it is too late. Top managers should meet their major customers regularly to find out:

- candid feedback about product or service quality and reliability
- ways in which the overall service could be improved
- changing requirements of their major and most demanding customers which could present a timely opportunity for you, or a threat if simply ignored
- any additional tailor-made or high value added products or service opportunities you may explore
- how the two companies could work together in a partnership role rather than a customer and supplier relationship
- changes in the size of their markets, the impact of emerging technologies, changes in their supply chain management and distribution channels which could affect your business.

In the same way, there are benefits to be gained by top management meeting key suppliers and pursuing a similar agenda in reverse.

Become known to headhunters

Probably the best time to make initial contact with headhunters is when you demonstrably are not looking for a job or do not even wish to consider changing jobs. So do your homework by visiting websites and contact relevant companies to find out which individual consultants are most relevant to meet. The next step is to suggest an exploratory meeting, at a time which suits the consultant, and to use the opportunity for a 'get to know you' chat and to outline your career objectives.

When headhunters make unsolicited contact with you, however, and if the opportunity described is not what you are seeking, or the timing is simply wrong, say so and explain your career objectives and timing. If you feel that it would be advantageous to meet the consultant, however, suggest a meeting for this purpose.

Become a magnet for other people

When people have this knack, it is obvious to others and an understandable reason to be envious. Charm, charisma and personal magnetism are not easily acquired online or by distance learning. Nonetheless, there are simple things which can be done to improve these qualities, including:

- be innately polite and courteous to everyone and avoid ever embarrassing anyone
- take a genuine interest in everyone you meet, be an interested listener and ask questions to learn more about the other person
- be well informed about the widest possible range of subjects and topical issues so that you can sustain a conversation on the topics raised by others
- avoid boring people by repeating anecdotes, waffling or riding your conversational hobby horses
- remember that interesting people do interesting things, and thus make interesting conversationalists
- people enjoy the company of people who smile, laugh and are inevitably cheerful; those who complain about their problems, illnesses and misfortunes understandably turn people off

- if you find it difficult to find topics for conversation, make a point of thinking up what you will raise in advance.

The area of knowing me, knowing you is about internal and external relationships in your working life. Good intentions are not enough, so complete the following action plan now.

KNOWING ME, KNOWING YOU ACTION PLAN

Date ______________________________

Get feedback

Manage your boss

Manage your business bank manager

Manage your private equity house

Manage your professional advisers

Manage your major customers and clients

Become known to headhunters

Become a magnet for other people

CHAPTER

08

MANAGE YOUR HEALTH

08

Whatever you do or avoid, there can never be any guarantees about your health. The corollary of this can never be to regard health as an inevitable lottery. A combination of sensible living, moderation and balance will pay huge dividends. Neither does it mean that the price of living longer and good health is to live in misery. Loss of good health, a lack of mobility, or suffering pain from illness are causes of misery.

An effortless way to improve your health is to adopt appropriate habits and routines. The best time to learn these is from babyhood. A taste for sweets, sugary and fatty food is developed alarmingly early in life, but parents have the chance to regulate this. Developing the habit of plenty of fresh air and exercise needs to be established in early childhood. Television and playing computer games need to be rationed. Cleaning teeth after meals is yet another habit to develop as early as possible. If you know that you do have some unhealthy habits, however, do not despair because it is never too late to change.

Weight

The latest official medical statistics from the USA classify 30 per cent. of the population to be obese. Whilst comparable figures for the rest of the world are likely to be lower, a high percentage of people are definitely overweight and their health would benefit from losing some weight.

Before deciding to lose weight, which will require a change in your diet and/or start taking more exercise, you are strongly advised to visit your doctor. The evidence is overwhelming that sudden weight loss is likely to be temporary and can damage your health, so reject any notion of pursuing a crash diet. Your best chance of lasting weight loss is to gradually lose weight, perhaps as little as half a kilogram per week, over a reasonable period during which time you have developed healthier eating habits and are taking more exercise. Using a suitable app on your phone can be helpful.

Diet

Eating the same foods, but in smaller quantities, inevitably means that when you stop 'dieting' the weight is likely to return. The aim should be to change your diet, and this does not necessary mean that you are continually feeling hungry.

Foods to avoid or to regard only as an occasional treat include:

- fried foods
- fatty foods
- chocolates
- sweets
- potato crisps
- cakes
- cream
- thick sauces
- biscuits
- soft drinks

If this sounds draconian, do not despair. Even some compromises are better than doing nothing, for example:

- choose lean bacon rather than streaky
- grill bacon rather than fry it, and place it on paper towel to absorb any surface fat
- use low fat oven ready chips rather than deep frying
- use low fat cream instead of full cream
- choose low fat products such as biscuits and crisps, but recognise the sugar or fat content is still likely to be quite high
- scramble eggs rather than fry them

Foods to eat in moderation include:

- red meat
- eggs
- processed foods
- cheese
- creamy dressings and sauces
- offal
- butter
- coffee

Processed foods include tinned and frozen products which may contain surprisingly high quantities of sugar, salt or fat.

Foods which are good for you include:

- salads
- fruit
- vegetables, including potatoes
- fish, especially oily fish such as salmon and mackerel
- pasta, but avoid thick, creamy sauces
- bread
- cereals
- beans
- lentils
- white meat

Potatoes should be boiled or baked, not sautéed or roasted. Ideally, meat and fish should be grilled. Bread should be brown or wholemeal rather than white. Olive oil is healthier than processed salad dressings. Basically you should eat plenty of fruit and vegetables every day as they are unlikely to increase your weight.

Monitoring your weight loss needs an accurate set of bathroom scales, but only check your weight once a week as to do it daily is unrealistic and unduly anxious.

Exercise

It really is important to visit your local doctor before embarking on an exercise programme. Plunging headlong into vigorous exercise can be harmful to your health, and may result in painful pulled muscles and suchlike.

Exercise abounds in good intentions, and many people quickly fall by the wayside. Even joining a gym club may result in an initial burst of regular exercise which soon wanes. The key to exercise is that it should be regular, enjoyable and result in breaking into a sweat but not finishing exhausted. Getting into the habit of regular exercise is important, such as the following:

- every morning before you shower, do an aerobic exercise routine or spend time on an exercise cycle, a rowing machine or a treadmill. You can even take the opportunity to watch the morning news on television whilst you are exercising
- every morning when the weather is dry, get off the train or bus a kilometre or two before your usual stop and walk to work
- similarly, use your lunch break to take a brisk walk
- always walk briskly up and down the stairs at work instead of using lifts. Better still, occasionally walk up and down several floors purely for exercise
- when choosing a gym club pick one close to your office so that you can visit before work, because there are always built in excuses and distractions at lunchtime or at the end of the day
- if your gym club is close to home, and doesn't open before you leave for work, make a point of visiting on your way home, because once you get home then it requires a greater effort to go out again to the gym

- provided your general fitness is good enough, jog or cycle to and from work regularly
- choose a game you enjoyed playing at school and join a team which plays primarily for exercise and enjoyment such as five-a-side soccer or hockey or cricket
- join with friends in a regular social game of tennis or squash

Sleep

As has been outlined earlier, adequate sleep is important for good health. Sleep repairs both the body and the mind. The immediate effect of inadequate sleep is not only tiredness, but reduced work effectiveness, poor concentration and the increased risk of accidents especially when driving. The effect of continued lack of sleep is to risk undermining your health and to make you more vulnerable to infection and illness.

A pragmatic test of sufficient sleep is that you should wake up feeling physically and mentally refreshed. The amount of sleep people need varies, and often reduces with older age, but many adults need at least seven hours sleep a night. In a way, you have a bank account for sleep. When a late night means that you have had too little sleep, top up your sleep account by having a brief sleep during the next day or ensuring you have ample sleep the following night.

Some executives are prone to macho displays of coping with sleep deprivation after an overnight long haul flight by working through the following day. Mental powers and concentration are significantly diminished, and worse still, the effects of jet lag may last for several days. It is much better to take a bath or shower, and benefit from a relaxed day spending time in sunlight, or at least enjoying fresh air, and doing some gentle physical exercise, all of which will minimise the effect and duration of jet lag.

Many people sleep much sounder and longer on holiday than when working, for the simple reason that the combination of more fresh air, exercise and a relaxed mind are powerful and natural sedatives. The inability to get to sleep quickly and easily or waking up early already thinking about work or personal problems cannot be allowed to continue. If increased fresh air and exercise, together with deliberate mental relaxation before trying to sleep do not cure the problem, medical advise is required. Sleeping pills should be regarded as only a temporary solution, because they can quickly become addictive or at least a necessary crutch and often leave people feeling jaded for a period after waking up.

Stress management

Stress comes from within, caused by external circumstances and pressures. Whilst acceptable levels of stress are quite healthy and normal, undue stress is harmful and potentially seriously damaging. Stress is a major issue in the workplace, and increasingly employers are addressing it constructively. Stress is indiscriminate, and can affect literally everyone from the chief executive to a recently joined college leaver. Absenteeism can be financially costly for companies in the following ways:

- many staff take occasional days off work, citing a minor illness, when the truth is that they cannot face work that day because of the stress
- staff may have to be 'instructed' to take, say, two weeks paid leave to avoid a mental breakdown
- a mental breakdown may involve a lengthy absence from work, with the inevitable disruption, and result in the person returning to work only able to perform a less demanding job

- in extreme cases, the person will be unfit to return to work and expensive compensation will result, or even litigation

Every manager and supervisor must be equipped to watch out for signs of stress. The cause may be work related or may result from external circumstances, but job performance and health are likely to suffer in both cases. The manager or supervisor needs to act quickly by sympathetically enquiring if there are problems, either at work or outside, which should be tackled. If necessary, the person must be urged to visit either their local doctor or a company medical adviser. Subsequently, it may be necessary to provide stress counselling, and increasingly companies use specialist stress counsellors on an ad hoc basis.

For the individual, when stress begins to reach unacceptable levels at work, the most sensible course of action is to raise the matter with your immediate manager. All too often, people suffer in silence when the problem is easily overcome by more equitable work sharing, some additional training or, if necessary, arranging a job transfer internally.

For someone suffering stress, symptoms which require urgent medical help include:

- working excessive amounts of overtime and, not surprisingly, failing to cope any better with the problems or workload
- increasingly 'shuffling work around', rather than tackling it effectively, and falling further behind
- an inability to concentrate and focus on work effectively
- a tendency towards rambling and incoherent conversation
- an inability to switch off mentally
- problems getting to sleep and/or waking up early already in a mental turmoil
- an increasing consumption of alcohol or drugs

Relaxation techniques

Some people find they benefit enormously from regularly using relaxation techniques, while others dismiss them as pure bunkum. At the simplest level, breathing and gentle stretching exercises can be helpful to people who are stressed or physically wound up. On the other hand, ancient techniques such as yoga and tai chi are based upon established techniques and proven principles.

If you have difficulties relaxing, then the familiar message is to find out more by visiting websites, reading books and magazine articles. Alternatively, there are yoga and other specialist classes widely available, and individual training by a personal coach as well.

Create work-free periods

It is not enough to be able to switch off from work, the rule should be to create regular work free periods when you do switch off completely. If you are unable to organise your working life so that every weekend there is one day when you simply forget about work, something is wrong. It suggests a marked workaholic trait. Your goal should be that as a routine you do not visit the office at the weekend, the only exception would be when there is a particular deadline to be achieved or a one-off task to be completed urgently.

Mobile 'phones are intrusive. If you find that you are receiving incoming calls regularly on Saturdays and Sundays, there is a simple remedy. Switch your work mobile 'phone onto voicemail, and buy another mobile for personal calls.

Leisure and holidays

Your non-working time should be at least as enjoyable and fulfilling as work. It is barren and boring simply to take time off from work and to do very little. Those people who either boast or admit that they would not know how to fill their time on retirement, need to start remedying the problem right away. Decades ago, retirement happened predictably between the ages of 60 and 65. Nowadays, enforced retirement can happen when people are in their 40s or 50s, because they simply may not be able to get another job which they are prepared to accept.

Leisure time should be enjoyable, active, social and varied. Active is not meant to suggest undue physical exercise, but it does reject spending long periods watching television or casually surfing the internet. Social means spending time with family and friends, and enjoying the company of other people by playing sport, a shared hobby or special interest groups. If your work is achievement orientated and competitive, leisure activities may well play down competitive activities.

Holidays are an essential part of personal health management. Your full holiday entitlement should be planned and taken. Spending holidays at home, doing very little may save money but it is a waste. Regard the cost of holidays as an investment. If you find it takes several days to wind down on holiday, that is a clear signal you are leading an unduly stressful life. Take two or three weeks continuous holiday so that you do manage to switch off and relax.

A holiday should provide a complete break from work and a change of routine. Whether it is a beach holiday or strenuous mountain climbing, you should return physically and mentally rejuvenated.

Alcohol

Alcohol is enjoyable, furthermore current medical evidence is that it is probably healthier to have a glass or two of wine a day, particularly red, than to be teetotal. Moderation is crucial, even if it is boring. Alcohol addiction creeps up on people. The recommended guidelines of not more than 21 units a week for men (a unit is a medium-sized glass of wine or half a pint of lager) and 14 units a week for women should not be exceeded.

Possible signs of alcohol addiction include:

- thinking about your first drink of the day almost from the time you awake
- finding an excuse to take your first drink even before bars and public houses open, perhaps by adding a shot of whisky in your coffee
- drinking when you are alone in the house
- secret drinking when family members tell you that you are drinking excessively
- a tendency to keep on drinking until the bottle is empty
- violence and abusiveness caused by drink
- rewarding yourself with a drink whenever things are not going well
- having a stiff drink before going out in order 'to get in the mood'

Alcoholism causes some people to lose their career, their partner, their children and their home, in a process which can be thoroughly degrading. Alcoholism is for life. Very few alcoholics, if any, succeed in being able to drink in a controlled way once they have overcome their excessive drinking. One alcoholic drink is often sufficient to trigger the problem again. So the message should be quite clear, if you are regularly exceeding the recommended limit or are showing signs of possible alcohol dependence, either reduce your drinking if you can or immediately seek medical advice and help. Delay is potentially unthinkably dangerous.

A simple way to demonstrate that you are not dependent on alcohol is to have at least one alcohol free day a week or to occasionally have an alcohol free week or month. If it will help, persuade a friend to do the same and stiffen each other's resolve.

Smoking

Smoking cannot be justified or defended. Smoking causes many premature deaths and widespread illness. Cutting down consumption is not an option, because there is a strong likelihood any reduction will only be temporary. Waiting to make a New Year's resolution is unacceptable delay. Take action now. The first step should be to consult your doctor. Products such as nicotine patches have helped many thousands of people to stop smoking.

Drugs

Cannabis may be harmless and may not be addictive; seemingly it is only a question of time before more countries will legalise the personal use of cannabis or at least de-criminalise it. On the other hand, some drugs are addictive or dangerous or both. The expressions 'social drugs' and 'social drug taking' are a complete misnomer. Ecstasy has killed people and cocaine is addictive. If the pressure of work causes you to take drugs, change your job. If drug taking is commonplace amongst your friends and you feel pressured to join them, change your friends. Drugs are a crutch which can and should be discarded now. Medical advice and help is available, substitute products are available to help overcome dependency, residential clinics provide help to deal with addiction.

Gambling

Occasional gambling is fun and not harmful. Millions buy lottery tickets every week and will never become remotely addicted to gambling. It is a fact, however, that gambling can become addictive and does wreck lives. One sign of a growing gambling problem is when someone is gambling and losing more than they can afford even without some aspect of their life suffering. Your local doctor will provide advice and access to counselling or Gamblers Anonymous as appropriate. People with a gambling problem must be urged to seek professional help without delay.

Retirement

People take it for granted that they will train and plan throughout their working life, which may well last for 30 years, for retirement. Given present life expectancy, and the rapidly growing trend of people retiring in their 50s, or even 40s, many people face 20 or 30 years or more of retirement. Financial planning is essential, but not enough.

Retirement can be forced upon people unexpectedly and suddenly in their 40s. For someone whose prime social contact has been with work colleagues and leisure time has been spent recovering from the stress of work, retirement will cause a huge void. Some employers provide training courses for people approaching retirement, and quite rightly for their partners as well. Some people simply cannot cope with retirement and find themselves bored, lonely and unfulfilled.

As retirement can be just as long as a working life, arguably it requires serious planning and preparation. Some people may ease themselves into retirement by switching to part-time employment if the company will agree, or seek a low level part-time job in order to fill some of their time even though they do not need any additional income.

On the other hand, people who make a success of their retirement are physically fit, happy and fulfilled to the point that they truly wonder how they ever had time to have a full-time job. Retirement should contain mental stimulation, social contact and appropriate physical activity.

Golf provides physical activity and social contact, whilst bridge or chess can provide mental stimulation and social contact. Bowls, both outdoors and indoors, can be enjoyed into old age and provides gentle exercise. Tennis can be played into the 70s, albeit at a slower pace.

Charity and voluntary work can provide a combination of mental activity and new friends. Learning, either to obtain a qualification or to learn a new skill, can achieve the same combination.

Retirement should be seen as an opportunity to grapple with technology, not to shun it. Computer courses for absolute beginners, and ones designed especially for the over 50s are widely available. Alternatively, find a personal computer trainer to give you practical tuition in the privacy of your own home. The Internet, emails and e-commerce can open up a whole new world.

The message should be clear, if you could be within five years of retirement, start planning and take action now to make the most of the opportunity ahead.

Mental attitudes

Positive mental attitudes have a favourable impact on your life, and probably contribute to better health. The most important one is self-esteem. High self-esteem is often accompanied by high achievement, fulfillment and happiness. Whilst a low self-esteem undermines achievement and contentment because of self doubt.

In simple terms, self-esteem requires liking yourself. Everyone can find things about their body appearance, habits and personality they are unhappy about. As the popular song says 'accentuate the positive and eliminate the negative' is the approach to adopt. Reinforce your self-esteem by rehearsing your achievements and favourable attributes.

Other mental attitudes to develop include:

- being positive rather than negative, and optimistic rather than pessimistic
- smiling frequently and being cheerful rather than having a reputation for being grumpy
- having an inner self-belief and self-assurance rather than self-doubt
- displaying poise, especially under pressure, and never being guilty of uncontrolled outbursts
- being spontaneous, open and straightforward rather than guarded and introspective

Health is so important that your next step should be to devise an action plan.

HEALTH MANAGEMENT ACTION PLAN

Date ______________________________

Weight

Diet

Exercise

Sleep

Stress

Relaxation techniques

Work free periods

Leisure and holidays

Alcohol, smoking, drugs and gambling

Retirement

Mental attitudes

CHAPTER

09

GET YOUR FAMILY AND SOCIAL RELATIONSHIPS RIGHT

09

Family and friends often end up at the bottom of the list of priorities for spending time. Work, sport, routine chores and study are likely to consume the overwhelming majority of time and energy. Just how shortsighted this has been may only become apparent when separation, divorce or bereavement occurs, and then it is likely to become obvious with a vengeance. Adequate time simply has to be made available for family and friends; you cannot afford to treat them as poor relations when giving your time to people.

Your partner or spouse

The saying that absence makes the heart grow fonder must be distrusted. The most commonly quoted reason given for failed showbusiness marriages is that working and living apart destroyed the relationship. If you spend all hours at work, and do not have any children at home, your partner may be lonely. When there are children to be cared for, your partner may feel imprisoned. Either way it could lead to a breakdown in the relationship.

The solution is neither complex nor secret. Like many things in life it requires common sense, some effort and balance. Tangible action which enhances personal relationships with a partner includes:

- make sure you remember birthdays, anniversaries and Valentine's Day. Cards need to be given at breakfast time, with a present which shows personal thought. A cheque, however generous, is unlikely to be as welcome as a thoughtfully chosen gift. If you are prone to forget, diarise the event to allow sufficient time to get a card and a gift
- celebrate birthdays and anniversaries on the actual date. When works gets in the way of the actual anniversary date, a celebration either before or after is likely to be viewed as second best

- when you are going away overnight on business, leave a card behind with a thoughtful message as well as telephoning home during your trip. Whenever possible, but not necessarily every trip, buy a small gift
- surprise gifts, even if small, show you care
- when arguments occur, as they inevitably do, avoid blame, insult and harsh words. The aim should be to understand your partner's point of view and the cause of dissatisfaction so that an agreeable way forward can be reached. Every attempt should be made to reach an amicable conclusion at the time. Sulking and not speaking are childish behaviour which cannot be excused. A good maxim is never to go to sleep without having resolved an argument
- bringing up past arguments or failings which have been put right is counterproductive and should be avoided. If an agreement to change a behaviour pattern does not achieve the desired change, however, then the subject should be raised again
- some couples spend a lot of time together and never really communicate. Effective communication in a partnership is not just about relating the events of the day to each other or discussing topical issues, important though these are. It is important to understand your partner's feelings and to be sensitive to any signals. When these occur, find out what is the cause. Better still, develop the habit of telling each other your anxieties, concerns and problems promptly
- make some time to talk to each other every day, free from the distractions of the internet, newspapers, television or any other distraction
- make a top priority of being there when you are really needed such as providing comfort for important medical appointments

Your parents

Parents can often be the forgotten relatives, especially when their adult children are juggling the priorities of work, home and a young family. Parents make sacrifices willingly for their children, and do not expect to be repaid later. The sad reality is, however, that some people only realise the situation when a parent dies prematurely or suddenly and then wish they had taken the opportunity to treat their parents differently or to have seen more of them. Simple things to do include:

- remembering birthdays and anniversaries for parents by a card and a gift is fine, but the gift of time is likely to be appreciated much more. Organise your life so that you can spend some time with them on their birthdays and anniversaries
- making landmark events, such as retirement, a special wedding anniversary or a landmark birthday, a day to remember. A party or event will need organising, but you are likely to find it equally rewarding
- inviting parents to spend part of Christmas with you, and especially for them to enjoy seeing their grandchildren opening presents
- arranging family holidays together, at least occasionally
- offering support when one parent dies, and recognising that loneliness may become a major problem. Birthdays and anniversaries can bring back the sense of loss, so be available to provide company and support. If loneliness is a problem, be available to talk through the situation and ensure that positive action is taken

Grandparents find visits from their grandchildren, and any great grandchildren, a source of joy and a special event to look forward to. So make sure that you find time to visit them or to invite your grandparents to visit you.

Your children

Parenthood does not come with a manual designed to ensure success, because indeed some people feel that they have done 'all the right things' only to see their children go off the rails. In truth parenthood means simple and rather obvious things, and hoping for the best, including:

- establishing basic ground rules as early as possible, without being disciplinarian, because children need to have behavioural guidelines
- teaching values and principles, which hopefully become second nature to them, by personal example. Remember that children often mirror their parents behaviour in adult life, for better or for worse, and this includes smoking, drinking, drug taking, dishonesty and violence
- providing the best possible educational opportunities compatible with a child's abilities and aptitudes. To send a child to an overdemanding school creates undue pressure and may result in a poorer level of achievement. Equally, to encourage a teenager to choose a prestigious and overly academic university compared to their ability is misplaced and selfish. Most children will achieve more in an environment suited to their aptitudes, interests and level of academic ability
- rationing the amount of screen time and monitoring use of social media, whilst encouraging children to play with other children and take physical exercise in the process
- recognising that a major benefit of nursery school is to learn social skills by playing with other children and any academic learning should be regarded as secondary
- encouraging and developing social skills such as politeness, good manners, courtesy, unselfishness, generosity, sharing and correct eating habits

- making time to spend with your children and to play with them
- attending birthdays, school plays, sports days, prize giving (especially if your child has not won a prize) and parents' evenings. It is inexcusable to allow work to get in the way except for unusual circumstances. Make a point of diarising every date as soon as you know it
- encouraging children to have an open mind and not to say they do not like something unless they have tried it and not foisting your personal prejudices onto them

Your other relatives

Family members can be a source of comfort and support in times of need. Invest time with siblings, cousins, aunts and uncles. Family get togethers do not have to be boring affairs. Take the initiative and organise an event which involves doing something together. Something as simple as a barbecue could be enjoyable. Similarly, hiring a boat for a river cruise should not be prohibitively expensive. All that is required is a little imagination.

Your friends and acquaintances

Making friends at work and spending time with colleagues socially can be enjoyable, but often much of this contact comes to an end or is sharply diminished on leaving or retirement. When colleagues socialise together conversation often centres around work or office gossip and usually is singularly boring and irritating for partners. Friends and acquaintances should provide an escape from work. Time and effort needs to be made to spend with existing friends and to make new ones. If you are mostly unavailable to accept invitations from friends, even for an informal drink, because work intervenes or you are otherwise committed, do not be surprised if eventually the invitations dry up.

Coping with separation and divorce

Separation and divorce are commonplace, but this does not make them any easier to handle. Divorce rates of about 40 per cent occur in many countries. In the UK the average length of a first marriage is only 10 years, and seven years for a second marriage.

Separation may just have happened to you, so the advice on your relationship with your partner contained earlier in this chapter may have come too late. Separation and divorce so often bring stress and unhappiness to both partners, and any children will suffer although it may not be apparent until considerably later. If the relationship was worthwhile and can possibly be restored, every effort should be made to do so. Counselling is widely available and has proved effective for many people. Sadly some people dismiss it out of hand, perhaps because they mistakenly think it is an admission of weakness.

Separation may be inevitable, however, and everyone should recognise that some people, men and women alike, are devastated by the experience. Furthermore, it is difficult to predict how well anyone will cope, because sometimes it is the most unlikely people who are devastated. Commonsense and practical guidelines for coping with separation and divorce include:

- recognising that even though one partner terminated the relationship, both people undoubtedly contributed to the situation

- acting coolly and calmly throughout, despite the temptation to retaliate and to provoke
- quickly making separate accommodation arrangements to avoid the confrontation likely to ensue from undue personal contact
- getting advice from any relatives and friends who have separated or divorced, because people without similar experience may well be singularly ill equipped to understand how you feel and to recommend what you should consider doing
- making sure that the best interests of any children are taken care of. Criticism aimed at the other parent or subjecting children to any form of tug of war can only be harmful. Children need reassurance and stability more than ever
- finding a suitable solicitor and ideally one that will do everything possible to achieve an equitable settlement without any undue provocation whatsoever. Provocation only produces retaliation and higher legal costs
- avoiding putting mutual friends into the invidious position of having to choose one partner or the other to support. Some people are likely to take sides, and sadly this has to be accepted when it happens, but things don't have to be this way. It is perfectly possible to maintain a friendship with both partners, albeit separately
- maintaining a relationship with your former partner to enable both of you to attend family events together and to share children's birthdays, school sports days and parents' evenings without any risk of acrimony

The fact remains, however, that some people are devastated, intensely lonely and unable to function properly at work. An experienced doctor gave the following advice for coping in these circumstances:

- live life only one day at a time, stop worrying about the future. Time is a great healer and although it seems that things will never get better when in the depths of despair, they inevitably will in due course
- seek to fill every day in order to minimise loneliness and despair. If necessary, temporarily work all hours in order to keep mentally occupied
- realise that people do not want to spend time with people full of self pity, but will gladly help people who are making an effort to overcome the situation
- avoid crutches such as sleeping pills, unless temporary and under medical supervision, excessive amounts of alcohol and drugs, because all of these will never solve the problem and could lead to dependency

This whole section on coping with separation and divorce may seem like an impossible counsel of perfection. This may be so, but in your heart you know it is sensible advice and, more importantly, it works.

Coping with bereavement and terminal illness

Everyone faces the difficult prospect of coping with a family bereavement at some point in life, and many will encounter a family member enduring a terminal illness. When either of these happens, the feeling may be one of temporary but absolute numbness of thought. Life has to go on, however, and this observation is not intended to be remotely callous or even insensitive.

The advice given earlier for coping with separation and divorce is equally applicable and effective. Bereavement counselling is widely available and has helped many people. Tears are understandable: grief needs an escape valve and no attempt should be made to hide it. Equally, talking about the departed person is an important part in coming to terms with death.

Terminal illness may seem tantamount to a prolonged period of helplessness, but this attitude is far removed from what can and should happen. Time is one of the greatest gifts to give. Personal ambition and a career should be put on hold at the very least, and if necessary leave of absence or part-time working must be negotiated. If your employer is unwilling to accommodate your need, be prepared to resign. An obvious priority is to secure the best possible care and treatment, but comfort, support and listening are personal gifts to be given generously. Hospices are fulfilling and inspirational places, positively focussing on the quality of life, and should be pursued as a valuable opportunity.

Finding a partner

For some people finding a partner is of overwhelming importance. Yet frustratingly, it is one of the things in life when to try too hard can be counterproductive.

Fortunately, finding a partner can happen in the most unlikely circumstances and when one is not remotely even thinking about it. To someone keen to find a partner, however, this may be of little comfort. There are positive steps one can take to maximise the chances, including:

- making the most of your appearance, refer to the relevant section earlier in the book
- joining a dating agency or a social group for single people, or using the internet, but some people will emphatically reject all of these
- pursuing group activities with like-minded people, and this is equally relevant at any age. Classes in conversational French or photography, the gym, tennis or hockey club are just a few of the countless opportunities to meet people which should be enjoyable in their own right
- displaying a positive mental outlook, refer to the relevant section earlier in the book
- becoming a better conversationalist. Taking an interest in current issues helps, and so does being aware of and interested in a wide range of subjects. Conversation is a technique in its own right, however, and the internet and books will provide practical tips

Gifts that count

This may seem a strange item to include in a chapter devoted to family and social relationships. Generosity is an attractive quality, but thoughtfulness can often be much more valuable and appreciated than the monetary value of a gift.

Some people have a genuine knack of choosing gifts which count, but it is something that can be learned. The starting point is knowing and understanding the tastes, likes and interests of the recipient. The direct way is to ask 'what would you really like me to buy you as a present?'. It should ensure that you buy something that is wanted, but lacks somewhat in subtlety. Somewhat better is to ask for a few ideas or pointers. Actively and continuously listening and looking for ideas and signals long before the time comes to buy a present is the ideal way.

To buy a gift for the home requires consciously being aware of the taste, style and colour schemes which the person has already chosen. To give a gift of clothing is a very personal thing to do, especially for the opposite sex, and there is a risk that it will scarcely ever be worn or regarded as downright unsuitable. The chances of getting it right can be increased by carefully observing the taste, style, look and colours favoured by the recipient.

Some people have the knack of choosing exciting or unusual gifts, but again one has to be able to anticipate the response of the recipient. Exciting presents include activities such as a ride in the London Eye, a journey by steam train, a parachute jump, a session driving a rally car on a race track. The list is endless, it requires thoughtfulness and a little imagination.

One test of a successful gift is that the recipient regards it as a treat or luxury they would never have bought for themselves. Another successful gift is the unusual item. People who seem repeatedly to manage to find unusual and desirable gifts make a point of continuously looking out for unusual items and know that the place to find unusual gifts is in individual shops rather than multiple stores.

As before, the only way to handle your family and social relationships better is to commit to taking action with the help of the following action plan.

FAMILY AND SOCIAL RELATIONSHIPS ACTION PLAN

Date____

Your partner or spouse

Your parents

Your children

Other relatives

Friends and acquaintances

Coping with separation and divorce

Coping with bereavement and terminal illness

Giving gifts that count

CHAPTER

10

THE NEW YOU: A PERSONAL VISION STATEMENT

10

A personal vision statement is a written description of the lifestyle you want to be enjoying at a given point in the future. This may seem an irrelevant waste of time, but that view is far removed from the truth. Repeatedly picturing and imagining the lifestyle you want in your mind's eye will dramatically help to make it happen. Furthermore, you have to really believe it will happen, really want it and really be determined to make it happen. 'Repeatedly' is a vitally important word too, because you need to remind yourself of and mentally rehearse your vision frequently. Ideally every single day.

Timescales are important because:

- within one year you can materially change some aspects of your life
- within three years some substantial improvements and achievements can be made to your life
- in five to ten years, you can transform your lifestyle beyond your wildest dreams, prior to reading this book, achieve wealth, fulfillment and happiness, and feel confident that you will cope with whatever life throws at you.

Your most powerful weapon to achieve this is your subconscious mind. It will 'lock on' to your personal vision and relentlessly steer you towards realising your vision.

Hopefully by now you are fired up with the belief and commitment to make your vision become a reality. The next step to make it happen is to write your personal vision statements as follows:

- short-term – one year ahead
- medium-term – three years ahead
- longer-term – within five to ten years

SHORT-TERM PERSONAL VISION STATEMENT

Date ____

Career and/or own business

Personal finances

Wealth creation

Health

Appearance and image

Self development

Relationships

Leisure

Mental attitudes

Reinvention

Retirement

MEDIUM-TERM PERSONAL VISION STATEMENT

Date ____

Career and/or own business

Personal finances

Wealth creation

Health

Appearance and image

Self development

Relationships

Leisure

Mental attitudes

Reinvention

Retirement

LONGER-TERM PERSONAL VISION STATEMENT

Date ____

Career and/or own business

Personal finances

Wealth creation

Health

Appearance and image

Self development

Relationships

Leisure

Mental attitudes

Reinvention

Retirement

CHAPTER 11

RECORD OF PERSONAL IMPROVEMENT/ ACHIEVEMENT

11

By now, hopefully you will have created goals and action plans which will bring you the achievement, lifestyle, fulfillment and happiness you really want.

The last remaining step is the most vital one of all. Namely to record what you have done and what you have achieved. Everything you do and achieve will inspire you to do and achieve even more. Consequently, this book should be kept readily accessible to log your progress month by month and year by year.

Develop the habit of faithfully reviewing what you have done and achieved every single month. Sound progress will motivate you, and should you find yourself backsliding then hopefully a record of inadequate progress will spur you on. A record table is included for each of the eleven major areas of improvement and achievement. Good luck.

Career improvement and achievement

Date	Action taken	Results achieved

Personal finances

Date	Action taken	Results achieved

Wealth creation

Date	Action taken	Results achieved

Health

Date	Action taken	Results achieved

Appearance and image

Date	Action taken	Results achieved

Self-development

Date	Action taken	Results achieved

Relationships

Date	Action taken	Results achieved

Leisure

Date	Action taken	Results achieved

Mental attitudes

Date	Action taken	Results achieved

Reinvention

Date	Action taken	Results achieved

Retirement

Date	Action taken	Results achieved

APPENDIX

'TOUCHSTONES' – HABITS AND TRAITS OF THE SUCCESSFUL

Successful people

Career

- Are resultaholic not workaholic
- Think and talk strategically
- Display leadership at every opportunity
- Are a demonstrable and unselfish team player
- Seek to embrace and utilise new technology
- Create and action a personal PR programme
- Develop financial skills

Health

- Pursue a healthy diet
- Regard exercise as important
- Drink in moderation
- Recognise and respond to stress symptoms
- Reject smoking and drug taking
- Get away for holidays and switch off
- Have a weekly work-free day

Relationships

- Realise effective relationships need time and candid communication
- Diarise important events such as birthdays, anniversaries, school sports days
- Always say thank you promptly
- Make other people feel good and appreciated

- demonstrably listen to and seek to understand people's viewpoint
- Resolve differences rather than ignore them
- Give gifts which show thoughtfulness

Personal finances

- Get on the property ladder
- Manage debt effectively
- Save and invest early in life
- Invest in pensions
- Plan to make paid employment optional
- Consider charitable giving
- Write a Will

Mental attitudes

- Think positively and always see a half-full glass not a half-empty one
- Never worry or agonise over things that can't be changed
- Develop a healthy self-esteem and self-image
- Believe their goals will be achieved and wholeheartedly commit to them
- Eliminate potentially harmful habits
- Display poise and inner self-confidence
- Maintain self control whatever the situation

Image and appearance

- Dress to reflect and help to achieve their future aspirations
- Pay attention to their speaking voice
- Are effective public speakers
- Greet people warmly
- Display poise
- Eliminate irritating habits
- Develop their charisma

Entrepreneurs

- Devote time to develop ideas for starting a business or getting an equity stake
- Identify and pursue the jugular vein opportunity
- Swim with the tide of opportunity, not against it
- Recognise that commonplace services and products can be branded, e.g. Kwik Fit and Pret à Manger
- Turn infrastructure needs arising from new technology into business opportunities, e.g. website design
- Research the marketplace and ideas rigorously
- Reward people generously for achieving demanding goals

Other titles by Thorogood

Great Leaders - Inspirational Lessons in Leadership

John Adair

Paperback ISBN: 978 185418 9172
Ebook ISBN: 978 185418 9189

John Adair asks, who are the great leaders in history and what have they got to teach us today about the nature and practice of leadership? In asking to what degree true leadership can be identified and developed, he explores the make-up and achievements of leaders as diverse as Lao Tzu and Machiavelli, Margaret Thatcher and Mandela.

Using a thematic structure, John Adair illustrates different facets of leadership, and examines the very different styles of leadership; he explores the cardinal qualities of inspiring, communicating and decision making but he also touches on the value of humour, intuition and imagination.

This is a thought-provoking book, rich in example and wide-ranging in scope: key qualities that so often appear abstract ideals – motivation, communication, decision-making, inspiration – here almost literally come to life.

The Best of John Adair on Leadership and Management

Edited by Neil Thomas

Paperback ISBN: 978 185418 9196
Ebook ISBN: 978 185418 9202

Here in one book is a brilliant summary of all John Adair's ideas, advice and techniques. The book is a clearly written master-class on:

- Growing into an effective and inspiring leader
- How to build a cohesive and responsive team
- Techniques of creativity and innovation
- Effective analysis and decision-making
- Mastering the art of good communication
- Managing your own time, managing yourself

The book is packed with practical guidance and insights, helpful charts, diagrams and forms.

The Concise Adair on Leadership

Edited by Neil Thomas

Paperback ISBN: 978 185418 9219
Ebook ISBN: 978 185418 9226

This book is a master-class on the art of leadership. While management fads come and go John Adair's work remains a beacon of practical advice and shrewd insight. This book encapsulates his writing on how to develop your own leadership potential, to motivate your colleagues and to build a creative and high-performance team.

The Concise Adair on Communication and Presentation Skills

Edited by Neil Thomas

Paperback ISBN: 978 185418 9233
Ebook ISBN: 978 185418 9240

There are many books on communication but few writers share John Adair's wide experience of management and leadership development in both business and military spheres. His knowledge and experience adds a rarely found depth and insight to hard-edged, practical techniques. This book encapsulates his writing on the art and skills of effective communication so you, whether you're at the beginning of your career or looking for a refresher, can put the techniques to best use.

The Concise Adair on Creativity and Innovation

Edited by Neil Thomas

Paperback ISBN: 978 185418 9257
Ebook ISBN: 978 185418 9264

This book is a goldmine of practical advice and shrewd insight. John Adair summarises everything you need to know in order to understand creative processes, eliminate obstacles and build on good ideas. He provides techniques to build confidence in your own creative skills and also gives practical advice on how to tolerate uncertainty and participate creatively as a team member or leader. In short, learn how to innovate and put great ideas into action.

The Concise Adair on Teambuilding and Motivation

Edited by Neil Thomas

Paperback ISBN: 978 185418 9271
Ebook ISBN: 978 185418 9288

This book encapsulates John Adair's writing on teambuilding and motivational skills in one easy to refer to master-class. These skills are of crucial importance in business and the leadership role in particular. Managers and leaders must be effective team builders and motivators to be able to achieve their business aims and get the best out of people. This book develops Adair's classic theory on Team, Task and Individual, and summarises all his writing on leaders and motivation and getting the best from people. It includes sections on being self-motivated, selecting people, target setting and reward and recognition.

The Concise Adair on Time Management and Personal Development

John Adair and Melanie Allen

Paperback ISBN: 978 185418 9295
Ebook ISBN: 978 185418 9301

John Adair's wide experience of management development adds a depth of insight and context to the practical advice in this book. It covers practical advice and skills on how to establish clear long-term goals and link your daily action planning to their achievement. It provides the tools, techniques and framework for continuing personal development so you can build a truly successful career.

To see a full listing of all Thorogood books go to:
www.thorogoodpublishing.co.uk

All titles can be ordered via the Thorogood website or direct from Amazon.

As well as publishing books which are accessible, practical and of immediate value, we also provide business and legal training events to support your skills development and learning needs.

Falconbury

Falconbury specialise in skills development for individuals and teams across all types of organisations, large and small, public and private, domestic and international. We run a large portfolio of events in a variety of formats from five-day industry-specific 'MBA-style' programmes to one, two or three-day courses – all of which can be delivered face to face or via a webinar platform.

All our public courses can also be run as tailored programmes for organisations anywhere in the world via a webinar platform or at a location of your choice. The programmes can be 'off the shelf', or we can work with you to create a bespoke training solution to meet your exact needs.

Finally, we also offer individual coaching and event management solutions.

With over 800 internationally renowned presenters, trainers, consultants, industry leaders and authors as training partners, Falconbury can deliver an all-encompassing international training and consultancy service.

To see our full portfolio of events go to **www.falconbury.co.uk** or, to discuss your particular training needs, please call our team of training advisers on **+44 (0)20 7729 6677**. We look forward to working with you.

Management Forum

For over 30 years Management Forum has been an internationally renowned independent training company that organises professional conferences, seminars and in-house courses for the pharmaceutical, life science and intellectual property sectors. Our aim is to provide you with the highest quality events that update you with the very latest information and are relevant and important to both you and your company.

We pride ourselves on our links to the best and most knowledgeable expert speakers in your business sector. We believe in bringing you together with your peers in order to learn, engage, share and network with the very best, whether that's face to face or via a webinar platform.

We are experts in knowing the experts you will want to hear from and have been bringing you this expertise since 1983. To see our full portfolio of events go to: **www.management-forum.co.uk** or, to discuss your particular training needs, please call our team of training advisers on **+44 (0)20 7749 4730**. We look forward to hearing from you.

Printed in Great Britain
by Amazon

59772376R00130